A
History
of
Weapons

A HISTORY of WEAPONS

Crossbows, Caltrops, Catapults
& Lots of Other Things that
Can Seriously Mess You Up

by JOHN O'BRYAN
illustrations by BARRY ORKIN

CHRONICLE BOOKS
SAN FRANCISCO

Library of Congress Cataloging-in-Publication Data

O'Bryan, John.
 A history of weapons : crossbows, caltrops, catapults &
lots of other things that can seriously mess you up / by John
O'Bryan.
  p. cm.
 ISBN 978-1-4521-1054-7 (alk. paper)
 1. Military weapons—History—Miscellanea. I. Title.

U800.O355 2013
623.4'4109—dc23

2012020511

Manufactured in China

Book and cover design by Neil Egan
Typesetting and additional design by Liam Flanagan
Illustrations by Barry Orkin

10 9 8 7 6 5 4 3 2 1

Chronicle Books LLC
680 Second Street
San Francisco, California 94107
www.chroniclebooks.com

CONTENTS

INTRODUCTION

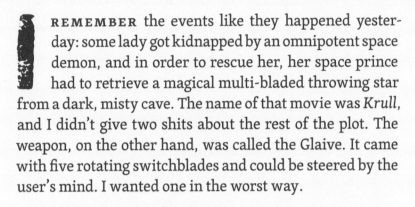

I REMEMBER the events like they happened yester-day: some lady got kidnapped by an omnipotent space demon, and in order to rescue her, her space prince had to retrieve a magical multi-bladed throwing star from a dark, misty cave. The name of that movie was *Krull*, and I didn't give two shits about the rest of the plot. The weapon, on the other hand, was called the Glaive. It came with five rotating switchblades and could be steered by the user's mind. I wanted one in the worst way.

But it was not to be. I would soon discover that the Krull throwing star was a Hollywood invention. The closest I could come was a three-inch shuriken that I convinced my mother to buy from a local weapons dealer (we lived in the rural South). I adored it and took it everywhere . . . until a Korean friend of our family told my mother that this throwing star could put someone's eye out. It was quickly taken away.

Then came the BB gun, every boy's first weapon. Mine was a fairly basic model. You could only pump it once, which meant it had limited power. But it packed enough punch to put holes in things like aluminum cans, particleboard, and my sister's ass. The BB gun was taken away from me, too.

Fast-forward 25 years, and what do we have? Me writing a book chock-full of every blade, club, and firearm ever to put a dimple on any-one's sister's backside. Well, maybe not every single one. For the sake of my sanity, I've had to prioritize. Every culture has a spear. Every culture has a bow and a dagger or saber or club of some kind. Some weapons didn't make the cut. The only weapons included are ones that I deemed interesting, unique, or important enough to take up book space. Remember this before you send me hate mail saying, "You forgot all about the tree pangolin trap of the Baka Pygmy tribe!"

Another thing I "forgot" is armor. This is a weapons book, and as such, it doesn't include entries on helmets, chain mail cuirasses, or any other protective clothing. The only shields you will find are ones that have a distinct offensive purpose, such as the Greek aspis or the crazier-than-batshit lantern shield. So if you're looking for *A History of Armor*, you'll have to look elsewhere.

You will also notice that this book ends around the time of the Spanish-American War. There are two reasons for this: (1) I had to stop somewhere. And since every war of the 1900s has already been covered to death by Steven Spielberg and Oliver Stone, what more can I really add anyway? (2) The point of this book is to have fun engaging your inner geek, not to make light of someone's tragedy. So I pussed out and decided not to cover Vietnam, nukes, or anything else that's "too soon." (My apologies to any readers who lost loved ones in the Spanish-American War—you must be really old!)

Rest assured, this book will still knock you all onto your collective ass. You will (hopefully) laugh, (probably) cry, and (God forbid) even learn a thing or two. In fact, people who read this book will undergo a transformation: Their IQ's will increase by at least twenty points. They will automatically gain the ability to wield battle-axes. This book can also cause the reader to grow a second pair of testicles, except for women, who will grow their first pair.

EASE OF USE KEY

Less than ★ - Easy! Even your cat could use it.

★ - Requires two opposable thumbs and as many brain cells

★★ - Requires depth perception and practice

★★★ - Sophisticated weapon; wielder must spend some time in the dojo

★★★★ - Only for masters

★★★★★ - Impossible; nobody but Bruce Lee and Batman could use it

Chapter 1.

THE FIRST WEAPONS

5,000,000–6000 BCE

OUR SPECIES has always been itching for a fight. Some say we started strangling each other with our fish fins as soon as we crawled out of the primordial ooze. It had to be that way. Without this instinct, we never would have made it out of the ooze in the first place. In fact, we humans (or something related to us) began murdering each other with weapons about five million years ago. We know this because we've observed chimpanzees using weapons, and they're roughly five million years behind us on standardized tests.

So what caused these early prehominids to make the leap to murdering each other with hand tools? Well, put yourself inside the feeble mind of this early man-ape. It's the beginning of the Stone Age, so obviously there are very few resources (other than an inexplicable surplus of stone). You can't *make* anything. You can't talk. You can't even keep yourself from standing in your own feces. You're not really out of apedom. You're a scavenger, feeding on nuts, berries, dodo bird eggs, shellfish, and anything else you can pick out of the dirt. But you've been walking upright for a while now, and that's freed up your front limbs. Before long you'll develop opposable thumbs, which allow you to pick up your feces before you step in it. Not only that, you can pick up lots of objects and throw them with greater dexterity. This opens up a whole new realm of possibilities—the realm of *throwing things at people who piss you off*. And boy, does it feel good!

ROCK

We can't say for certain, but we're pretty sure this was "the original." The Grandmaster Flash of weapons. The first object ever used to crack a person over the head. After all, it's heavy. It's hard. It fits in your hand perfectly. You haven't yet mastered rock propulsion via sling or learned to sharpen the rock to form arrows or spears. You aren't as fast, nimble, or strong as your would-be predators. But you do have something they don't: thumbs. This means you can find rocks and throw them with remarkable accuracy, sometimes even killing your target. Defending yourself against the more athletically gifted organisms is a full-time job. And as if dealing with lions and bears weren't enough, you've got to deal with competition from your fellow knuckle-draggers, who are constantly trying to steal your food (and your wife) while you sleep. But thanks to those opposable thumbs, you can use a rock to bash your adversary's skull when he's asleep and steal all of *his* nuts, berries, dodo bird eggs, and shellfish. Not only do you get to keep your wife—you get to take his as well. Now your DNA will be passed down to the next generation of hominids, while your adversary's will not. And it's all thanks to the rock.

EASE OF USE: ★★
(some calluses will result)
DATE OF ORIGIN:
Four billion years ago
PRECURSOR TO: Hand axe
BEST DEFENSE: Get out of the way!
USER REVIEWS: *"Grrrr...*
Rock *smash!* Make *dead!*
Thumbs *good!"*

FIRE

Early man knew the power of fire. He'd seen it spread naturally and devastate the landscape overnight. *Homo erectus* (the early hominid, not the gay porn film) wanted this power for himself. He would spend millennia attempting to harness it. Eventually, about 790,000 years ago, one of our knuckle-dragging ancestors succeeded. Whoever he was, this early man was known as Lord Bigshit in the caveman community. Thanks to fire, Lord Bigshit could keep wild animals at bay. He could use the fire to harden his rocks, making them even more effective at collapsing enemies' skulls. He could make light after the sun went down. And he could cook his shellfish before eating it, ensuring that he wouldn't be dead after dinner. But most importantly (for the sake of this book anyway), *Homo erectus* now had the power to wipe out large numbers of other cavemen. He could torch entire settlements in a matter of minutes, especially with fire codes not having been invented yet. He could also asphyxiate cave dwellers by pumping smoke into their domiciles. He could instantly turn anything to ash. Everyone wanted what Lord Bigshit had. His "hot red flower" was about to change the world forever.

EASE OF USE: ★★★★
(especially if you're rubbing sticks together)
DATE OF ORIGIN: 200,000 to 790,000 years ago
DISCOVERED BY: Lord Bigshit
COUNTER WEAPON: Water
USED WITH: Arrows, marshmallows

CLUB

Now picture yourself two million years ago. You've evolved slightly. You're now *Homo habilis*. (Think *Homo sapiens* with even *smaller* brains.) You don't have sharp claws, giant saber teeth, or poison quills like some of the other members of the animal kingdom, but you do have intelligence—just enough of it to turn anything into a weapon. That tree branch lying on the ground? A ready-to-use truncheon. That mammoth femur? Even better. (In fact, according to the noted historical source *2001: A Space Odyssey*, a bone was the first weapon ever used to commit homicide.) In the centuries before mankind learned the sophisticated art of stick sharpening, he relied on crude, blunt objects to do his bludgeoning. In the case of the club, its effectiveness hinges on its mass. The heavier the club, the more force it carries when you wield it. So swinging a tree branch at another creature isn't exactly sophisticated,

but it's more than the other beasts of earth can do. When was the last time anybody saw a lion pick up a club and whack a hyena? This ingenuity is precisely what made early man the real king of the jungle. Once he learned to swing a club, he could kill the lion and build several more clubs from its bones. In your face, lion.

EASE OF USE: ★★ (some strength required)
DATE OF ORIGIN: Two million years ago
MADE FAMOUS BY: Captain Caveman
PRECURSOR TO: Mace
NOT TO BE CONFUSED WITH: Club sandwich, which is not an effective weapon

STONE BLADES

So you're climbing the evolutionary ladder, and you've just begun to break the chains of apedom. You've spent a few millennia smashing things with rocks, and it's starting to dawn on you—some rocks have narrow edges that make it easier to saw through other objects. The principle of physics that you don't yet grasp is this: a force increases exponentially when it's distributed over a smaller surface area. Make the point of your weapon smaller, and you can actually cut somebody and spill his blood. You've just discovered *sharpness,* and the way you achieve it is by flaking bits of rock off a bigger rock by hitting it with a piece of antler. Hooray for technology! These rock blades took many shapes in the Paleolithic era: knives, wedges, spikes, etc. Most were made from flint, due to its predictable cleavage (write your own boob joke here). All started out as crude, hand-held blades. Sure, they got the job done. But

they were seriously lacking in style, and could also hurt the user's hand. One day, however, one of the smarter cavemen—probably their valedictorian—made a startling discovery: he could attach a piece of wood or bone onto the blade, and voilà . . . it's got a handle! This would usher in the hand axe, one of the most important tools of early hominids. Not only that, the new handle allowed the user to strike harder without injuring his tender hominid hands.

DATE OF ORIGIN: 1.5 million years ago
BIRTHPLACE: Kenya
INVENTED BY: *Homo habilis*
ALSO USED TO: Skin animals, cut uncomfortable tags off caveman T-shirts

OBSIDIAN
The Black Glass of Death

The sharpest blades in history were not made of steel. Oh, no. They were crafted thousands of years ago from a naturally occurring material called obsidian. This jet-black mineral forms in the lava flow of active volcanoes. The rapid cooling of this material means it solidifies with very few crystals. It's hard and brittle and therefore breaks into very sharp pieces. In fact, well-crafted obsidian blades are said to be many times sharper than modern surgical scalpels. I know what you're thinking, smart-ass— "If obsidian's so great, how come doctors don't make scalpels out of it?" Even though the edge it produces is second to none, obsidian isn't the most durable substance. It chips and loses its edge much more easily than any metal, so it has to be replaced frequently. It's also difficult to mass-produce, unlike metal items that are made from a mold.

Another drawback: it's only found near volcanoes, and most people prefer not to go anywhere near those. But if you were a guy who lived thousands of years ago and needed to slice someone open, obsidian was the way to go. Just ask the conquistadors who saw one of their horses decapitated by an Aztec obsidian blade. It's no wonder the Aztecs considered such a material to be sacred. Obsidian was also highly valued by the ancient Egyptians, who probably used it to cut open mummies and make shiny trinkets for their cat-gods to play with.

SPEAR

Now that you've got fire, you have the ability to harden wood and forge it into sharp points. It's taken your simian brain millions of years to figure this out, and the result is the spear. This is arguably the first serious weapon. Granted, it doesn't take much to learn how to sharpen a stick. Scientists in our time have seen chimpanzees stripping the bark from tree branches to use as weapons (once again supporting my theory that you should *never* fuck with a chimp). But once fire was added to the equation, spears became harder, sharper, and much more effective at penetrating flesh. Early man could now heat stones, making them easier to chisel into sharp blades and points. Some cultures, such as the pre-Columbian Mesoamericans, chiseled their spear tips from obsidian (see page 15). Rest assured, these early fire-hardened spears could cut through animal hide like a hot poker through an ice cream sundae. Alas, despite its awesomeness, the spear has all but vanished from modern arsenals. Though it is still utilized by certain primitive cultures, such as Ted Nugent.

EASE OF USE: ★★✦
DATE OF ORIGIN: Five hundred thousand years ago
MADE FAMOUS BY: Achilles, before he got one in the heel
BEST DEFENSE: Shield, armor
FUN FACT: As awful as it was to get stuck with a spear, it was even worse to see it pulled out with your guts on the end of it

BOOMERANGS & THROWING STICKS

When you think of boomerangs, you probably picture a V-shaped Australian object that magically returns to the hand of the sender. Or maybe you think of the three-pronged Nerf toy that always gets stuck on your roof. Fact: none of these returning boomerangs were intended to be used as weapons. *Never* go hunting with your Nerf boomerang. Another fact: *most* boomerangs were non-returning and were made exclusively to maim other people or animals. Non-returning boomerangs—and their older cousins known as throwing sticks—were typically used by ancient hunters to kill fowl and small mammals, but they saw action in combat as well. The "hooked" boomerangs, in particular, were said to be especially effective against shields, as they hooked the shield and swung around to the other side, knocking the opposing warrior senseless. Not all boomerangs were thrown. Some were used as clubs in hand-to-hand combat, some were used as scraping tools, and some were even used as musical instruments. And they weren't exclusively Australian, either. The oldest throwing sticks were used tens of thousands of years ago by primitive man in what is now Poland. They were also used by the ancient Egyptians to hunt ducks, and by ancient Native Americans to hunt rabbits (hence their other name, rabbit sticks). The throwing stick may have been the first weapon ever to be made airborne. It's also probably how humans first made friends with dogs.

EASE OF USE: ★★★ (throwing sidearm puts strain on your joints)
DATE OF ORIGIN: At least 23,000 years ago
MADE FAMOUS BY: Some Australian guy
USED WITH: Koala bear, didgeridoo

JAVELIN

Who hasn't watched the javelin throw during the Olympics and thought, "Man, I'd like to see that fucking thing kill somebody." Well, once upon a time, javelins did exactly that. Now, you might think that the spear and the javelin are the same thing. But you'd be dead wrong. Try to throw a spear, and you'll find yourself having to stand still and balance the shaft in your fingers. You're also likely to find that the spear is too heavy to throw very far. If this were a battle, you'd already be a casualty. The spear's primary purpose is to remain firmly in your grasp and serve as a melee weapon. Now pick up that javelin (assuming you have one nearby). It's much lighter, isn't it? And its weight is distributed differently, with the bulk of it lying in the tip. This front-heaviness allows it to become airborne, ensuring a much smoother flight. It also allows the weapon to be thrown on the fly. Javelins can be launched without having to plant your feet and find your balance. Eventually the Greeks and Romans would amend them with metal tips, making them even deadlier. In addition, a string called an amentum was sometimes wrapped around the shaft, allowing the hurler to put spin on the javelin and make it fly even farther. But the original javelin—the one that started it all—was born in the lower Paleolithic era some 400,000 years ago, long before the ancient Greeks thought of the Olympics. It was little more than a sharpened piece of throwable wood, but it put a lot of woolly mammoths on our ancestors' tables.

EASE OF USE: ★★★
PRECURSOR TO: Roman *pilum*
MADE FAMOUS BY: Hercules, who was the strongest guy ever, so of course he could throw the hell out of the javelin

BOLA (BOLEADORA)

When the Spanish conquistadors arrived in South America, they reported that they didn't trust the natives in this new land, partly because they fought with "arrows, and stone bowls that are fixed at the ends of a cord." Indeed, the South American Indians did use such a weapon (as did the Inuit and Chinese simultaneously), and that weapon was the bola. The concept began simply as a single rock on the end of a string, swung over one's head to build momentum and then released toward the target, hopefully crushing his skull. This "single-ball" bola would later become known as the *bola perdida*. One day the Indians of Las Pampas, Argentina, made a groundbreaking discovery: if you want to capture your prey alive, all you have to do is add more strings and a couple more weights. The result was a multipronged bola that could wrap up an animal's legs and *immobilize* it rather than kill it. This was an ideal tool for the South American gauchos, who spent their entire day herding cattle. North American cowboys may have had the lasso, but the gauchos had the much cooler bola.

EASE OF USE: If you don't mind injuring your target: ★★
If you want the target unharmed: ★★★
MADE FAMOUS BY: South American gauchos
PRECURSOR TO: Medieval flail;
tying someone's shoelaces
together

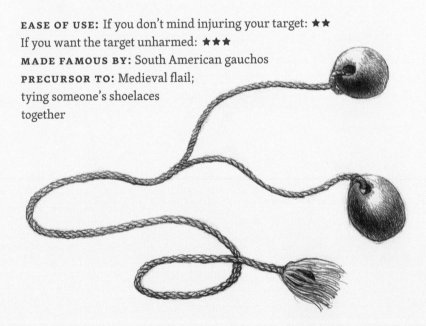

SLING

This simple strap of leather and cloth is another of mankind's first attempts at ranged warfare. Simply place a stone in the pouch, swing for momentum, and release. Bang! Instant dead giant. The concept is this: you can throw a rock much harder when you have a longer arm. The sling accomplishes this, essentially lengthening a person's arm and generating more power by centrifugal force. There are two basic slinging techniques: over one's head, or in an underhanded motion near one's waist. Whichever way you choose, the sling should always be swung hard enough to keep the straps taut. The stone is released with a whipping motion near the front of the orbit. Make no mistake—this can fuck a person up, and from a distance, at that. The range of a sling rock can even exceed that of an arrow from a bow. It's also cheap to make, and ammunition is found everywhere. But—let's face it—the sling has always been a pauper's weapon, even in ancient times. It has zero use in melee situations, and despite what you've heard in Sunday school, it isn't going to win many fights against a seriously armed opponent. Also, the immediacy of your attack goes out the window when you have to wind your weapon up by whipping it around over your head. It's a bit like trying to ambush somebody with a tetherball pole.

EASE OF USE: ★★★↓
USED WITH: Rocks, bullets
MADE FROM: Wool, flax
MADE FAMOUS BY: David, who allegedly brought down Goliath with a rock to the head
ADVANTAGES: Ammunition is plentiful
DISADVANTAGES: User must build momentum before releasing

DAVID & GOLIATH
The Real Story

A long time ago, there was a Philistine giant named Goliath. He was about the size of a grain silo and loved to taunt the Israelites. Goliath carried a spear, a javelin, and a sword, and he was covered from head to toe in bronze armor, save for a small piece of unprotected forehead (remember that for later!). For forty days he challenged the Israelites to send a champion to meet him in battle, and for forty days the Israelites cowered. Finally, a young man named David went to meet the giant's challenge with nothing but a sling. David was so sure of himself that he only bothered to collect five stones for his ammunition. Not only that, he refused to wear the king's armor. (Check out the balls on David!) David and the giant met on a field between two mountains. They shouted insults and threats at each other like a couple of rednecks in a bar fight. Goliath threatened to feed David to the birds, and David insulted Goliath's foreskin. Then shit got out of control. David pulled a stone from his pouch, placed it in his sling, and hurled it at the lone piece of uncovered skull on the giant's face. This pitiful attack made the giant laugh so hard that he fell right onto his spear. The moral of this story? The only way a scrawny, unarmored kid with a sling beats a ten-foot-tall giant covered in bronze is if the giant trips and falls on his spear. Believe it.

ATLATL

It's pronounced AHT-lah-tl, but you can call it "kicker of many asses." How many asses exactly? Put it this way: some anthropologists believe this ancient dart-thrower was the major culprit in wiping out the woolly mammoth. Like the sling, the atlatl acted as an extension of the arm, allowing the warrior to throw the projectile many times farther. It functioned much like the scooped ball-thrower you use to play fetch with your dog, only instead of throwing tennis balls, it threw deadly flesh-skewering darts. A crucial component to the design was the flexibility of these darts. The atlatl relied on its projectile bending during release, causing it to launch from its resting place like a spring. This design seems to have been ubiquitous, appearing all over the world in many places where the atlatl was independently invented. It is estimated that every culture on Earth has relied on the atlatl to hunt food at some point. Native Americans carried the atlatl across the Bering Strait during their mass migration. Ancient Europeans used it too, but then abandoned it in favor of the bow thousands of years ago. So when they invaded the New World centuries later, they had long since forgotten about this dart-throwing juggernaut. They were alarmed to see this primitive weapon in action, penetrating the mail armor of their conquistadors. These white old farts quickly decided it was time to write to their kings and request some lessons in the atlatl.

DATE OF ORIGIN: 21,000–40,000 years ago
BIRTHPLACE: Europe, Asia, Africa, Egypt, Australia
USED WITH: Atlatl darts (sold separately)
FAMOUS VICTIMS: Woolly mammoth, Spanish conquistador

NEOLITHIC BOW

The atlatl was king of Neolithic ranged weapons. In the right hands, its projectiles were deadlier than anything on the battlefield. But deadlier doesn't always mean better, and the atlatl was about to find itself in the world's first-ever format war—the VHS vs. Betamax battle of the prehistoric world. And just like in that battle, the superior format would *lose*, as people were willing to sacrifice quality for convenience. Ancient warriors loved the atlatl, but they ultimately found themselves looking for a way to launch missiles without putting so much strain on their shoulders. (*You* try throwing a few atlatl darts and see how your pitching arm feels afterward.) Sometime around the dawn of civilization, possibly up to forty thousand years ago, someone figured out how to make a bow. This crude mechanism was probably whittled from saplings and strung with animal guts. Its missiles couldn't travel as far as those of an atlatl, and its power was limited, especially in penetrating thick hide or clothing. But its ammunition (arrows) was much easier to make than the elastic darts of the atlatl. Arrows didn't need to bend, since all the necessary elasticity was stored in the bow. This meant Neolithic man could easily collect an entire quiver of arrows, as opposed to a handful of darts for his atlatl. So the atlatl became obsolete, leaving us to wonder what could have been. Just imagine how much cooler it would have been if William Tell knocked the apple off that guy's head with an atlatl, or if Cupid made people fall in love by nailing them with atlatl darts.

EASE OF USE: ★★★↗ (can take a lifetime to master)
DATE OF ORIGIN: 15,000–40,000 years ago
VARIATION: Pellet bow (shoots rocks instead of arrows)

Chapter 2.

IT'S SO MUCH EASIER TO KILL PEOPLE WITH METAL

4000–500 BCE

AFTER WANDERING in the wilderness for millions of years, *Homo sapiens* had finally begun to get his shit together. Literally. He now made his feces in a designated place, far away from his stored food. Perhaps as importantly, he now *had* stored food. *Homo sapiens* could grow his own crops. He even had the foresight to know there wouldn't be any crops in the winter, so he should put some away for later. In his free time, he domesticated a few animals. And he was beginning to do something else fancy: Develop complex mathematics. And written languages! "Welllll . . . looks like we got ourselves a reader," says one of the other apes.

But it wasn't all quiz bowls and spelling bees. Early man still hadn't shaken those ape genes completely. He continued to practice cannibalism like it was going out of style. He may have had relations with those animals he'd been domesticating. And he still performed human sacrifices by the truckload. So of course he needed weapons. It just so happened he'd discovered a brand-new metal for making those weapons . . .

Copper. Ancient man probably discovered this by accident, perhaps by unintentionally smelting some metal in a campfire. He later discovered that he could mold it into very precise shapes—with very sharp edges. This meant he could make tools. Hell, he could even mass-produce these tools. And that meant he could mass-produce weapons.

COPPER DAGGER

It's the start of the Bronze Age, and believe it or not, swords are not yet king of the battlefield. Metallurgy is still an infant science, and it has yet to produce anything stronger than copper. Copper has a lot of good qualities: It's durable. It's very malleable. It won't chip like stone. It can be mass-produced. It turns pretty colors with age. But it's soft (about as soft as limestone) and therefore doesn't hold its edge for very long. This means copper requires frequent sharpening. It's also slightly harder to come by than stone. So copper can't be used to make any practical blade longer than a dagger. This new metal dagger is no party favor, mind you. If placed correctly between the ribs, it can take out an unarmored opponent with relative ease. But as quality goes, the copper dagger is not a marked improvement over the flint or obsidian models. Why, you might as well be stabbing someone with a penny. In fact, if you own a copper dagger, you might find it's worth more as currency than as a weapon. Consider selling it to a precious metals dealer and using the money to buy one of those newfangled socketed axes.

EASE OF USE: ★
DATE OF ORIGIN: Early Bronze Age
(3000-ish BCE)
USED IN: Egypt, Mesopotamia, India
CAN BE RECYCLED INTO: Pennies, wiring

SICKLE-SWORD (KHOPESH)

The sickle-sword typically resembles a question mark, and that's probably exactly what people felt when they saw this strange, undulating blade coming for them. "Sweet Ra the sun god, what is that curved stick of metal coming at me?!" The *khopesh* was invented by the Sumerians and used against the Egyptians in battle. It left such an impression that Egypt would later adopt the sickle-sword in its own military. In fact, the Egyptians loved the khopesh so much that they would take it to the grave with them, burying it in the tombs of their rulers. As you might expect, the strange shape of the khopesh serves a practical purpose. The hook on the end of the sword allows the wielder to yank his opponent's shield out of the way. Once that's achieved, he can use the edge of the khopesh to hack the enemy to pieces. You could even speculate that the curve of the blade helps with reinforcement, preventing it from bending on impact. This was especially helpful in an era when everything was made from weak-ass copper. Occasionally, the end of the khopesh would be sharpened as well, providing a serviceable tip for stabbing, because hey—the Egyptians liked to keep things fresh.

DATE OF ORIGIN: 2500 BCE

LENGTH: 50-60 centimeters

TYPE OF DAMAGE: Mostly slashing; some stabbing

BEST DEFENSE: Arrows, slings, and other ranged weapons; also consider: armor

PRECURSOR TO: The *kopis*, a forward curving sword of Greek infantries; saber; scimitar

ALSO CALLED: *Sappara* (Assyrian); wicked shaap question maaak (Bostonian)

SOCKETED AXE

Once upon a time in the Fertile Crescent, in the ancient cities of Sumer, people discovered they had been using terrible, unreliable axes. This was largely becasue before the Sumerians, nobody knew an axe joint from their asshole. For thousands of years, people had been making their axes the same way. They would fasten the blade to the handle using lashings and rivets (basically rope and bolts). The head of the axe was heavy out of necessity, so it was often difficult to keep it on the shaft. The axe would fall apart in no time, often in midswing, and the axe head would go sailing off. The Sumerians grew weary of watching stray axe blades fly into bystanders' faces. Luckily for them, their local metallurgists had just discovered how to add tin to copper to make bronze—a stronger material for making arms. They also came up with a better design by molding the blade with a built-in socket. The new axe head and socket piece could slide right over the handle of the shaft and wedge into place. The axe head stayed safely on the shaft and didn't fly into their friends' heads. Problem solved!

DATE OF ORIGIN: 3000 BCE

BIRTHPLACE: Sumer

REPLACED: Lashing and rivets technology

NOT TO BE CONFUSED WITH: Axe body spray, a foul chemical weapon favored by eighth-grade boys

USER REVIEWS: "This new axe is amazing. It doesn't accidentally kill my children while I'm chopping firewood. Thanks, socketed axe!"

EGYPTIAN MACE

I've always thought of the mace as a rich man's version of the club. It packs all the blunt force of a crude Stone Age club, but it's designed and polished for the fashion-conscious warrior. The mace is normally bisymmetrical from tip to handle, sometimes adorned with knobs on the head. But the architectural beauty of this weapon belies its brutal nature. It was allegedly the first weapon designed specifically for killing humans, although the original mace was little more than a rock on the end of a stick. The weapon really didn't come into its own until Egypt, circa 3000 BCE. The Egyptians went all out, experimenting with mace heads of varying shapes: disc-shaped, pear-shaped, an even some shaped like the tops of halogen lamps. With the advent of bronze, the Egyptians found the perfect material for their mace heads. Bronze-plated maces could crack hundreds of skulls before falling apart. This was in stark contrast to their stone predecessors, which often shattered on the first kill. The mace requires relatively little skill and an incredible amount of strength. But if you find yourself up against a wall of soldiers in impenetrable scale armor, the mace is one way to solve the puzzle. Rather than attempt to pierce the bronze, the idea is to bash it to the point of denting or collapsing, shattering your opponent's bones in the process.

DATE OF ORIGIN: 3000 BCE
USED IN: Egypt, Mesopotamia, India
PRECURSOR TO: Flanged mace; morning star
ADVANTAGES: Can squash anything to a bloody pulp, even if it's wearing armor
DISADVANTAGES: Only used on people, which kind of ruins that whole "I only use it for hunting!" excuse

COMPOSITE BOW

The original bows were "self" bows, meaning they were comprised of a single piece of wood. This was fine until some cheating asshole showed up covered in bronze scale armor and ruined it for every archer this side of the Himalayas. Like the axe, the bow would need a serious makeover if it was to survive the age of metal. Fortunately, someone (this is debatable, but probably someone in the Middle East) had a serious stroke of genius. "What if . . . bear with me here, but *what if* instead of using just wood to make the bow, we add—call me crazy—animal guts, and then—wait for it!—*we slap on a layer of raw, uncut diamonds?*" Well, that turned out to be a pretty expensive endeavor, so they came up with a new material for the side facing the archer: animal horn. And the first composite bows were born! The layer of animal sinew brought elasticity to one side of the bow, and the layer of horn brought firmness and support to the other side. The result was a lot more energy stored in a relatively small bow—enough to pierce armor. The only drawback was the difficulty of maintaining such an elaborately crafted weapon. Humidity was the enemy of every composite bow. The layers were glued together (usually with more animal products), and moisture could cause them to fall apart. And nothing sucks more than trying to hot-glue your bow back together in the middle of a battle.

DATE OF ORIGIN: 2000 BCE

MADE FAMOUS BY: Egyptians, who may have gotten the idea from Asiatic nomads

PRECURSOR TO: Hunnic bow; Mongol recurve bow

USER REVIEWS: "I've got a composite bow. I don't need the Egyptian police to save me from intruders . . . except when it rains. Then I call the Egyptian police to save me."

THE CHARIOT

Remember how excited you were when you got your first car? That's probably how the ancient Mesopotamians felt when they built their first chariot. And just as we can admit with hindsight that our first car was a piece of shit, most people would say the same thing about the chariot. But in its day, the chariot was the equivalent of a Sherman tank. It rolled over infantries, gave mobility to archers, and changed the very game of warfare in Mesopotamia. And come to think of it, the chariot scene is the only part anyone remembers from *Ben-Hur*, so there's that. Most historians believe that the chariot was introduced to Egypt by the mysterious Hyksos invaders—who brought it over from the Fertile Crescent. Chariots were a huge factor in Egypt's defeat, and they would be in many battles to come. As if the chariot weren't already badass enough, some sadistic fuck thought of putting blades on the wheels. The scythed chariot, as it's known, was likely invented by the Persians. It made appearances at several famous battles near the end of the millennium. There is evidence that scythed chariots have been somewhat successful at breaking up infantry lines, and they may have taken out a fair number of opposing chariots in their time. But the primary purpose of these bladed war chariots was probably not to kill, but to terrify and demoralize. The way your neighbors were when your dad first gave you the keys to that Pinto.

EASE OF USE: ★★★ (Wheels can break; driving is rough. Roads not invented yet.)

DATE OF ORIGIN: 2500 BCE

BIRTHPLACE: Mesopotamia

OFTEN USED WITH: Wheel scythes, archers

PRECURSOR TO: Ford Pinto

Human Sacrifices
Somebody's Got to Pay for This Shit

You can imagine the following speech coming from some village elder four thousand years ago: "Look, we've all got to die someday. At least this way you'll die knowing you made the gods happy. Your death will bring us shitloads of rain for our crops. We'll think of you every time we eat wheat!" It sounds insane to us in the modern world, but ancient man didn't know *anything*. And since he didn't understand things like weather, he assumed there was probably something pretty powerful living in the sky. And whatever it was must be pretty angry. And it must be a *he*. And he *must want BLOOD*. After all, people need blood, so a god must need even more of it. So in cultures around the world, high priests got out their sacrificing daggers and went to work. We're not just talking Aztecs, either. Nearly every culture from Scandinavia to Egypt had some tradition of ritual murder. The Celts burned their sacrifices alive inside of a giant wicker effigy (the famous wicker man). The Mixtecs of Central America played a type of ball game against opposing cities. The rules were "loser gets sacrificed." (That's one way to make baseball interesting.) The Thuggee of India strangled unsuspecting travelers to appease Kali, the goddess of destruction. Even the biblical God Himself liked to trick the ancient Jews into sacrificing their young, only to stop them at the last minute and say, "Totally kidding! That was only a test." Oh, that Jehovah. What a prankster.

THE FIRST
BIOLOGICAL WEAPONS

Remember when your parents would make you play with a kid who had chicken pox, just so you'd catch the disease and get it over with? You could say this is a mild example of a biological weapon. Historians tell us that the first bio-warfare was employed several thousand years ago by the Hittites, an ancient people who found themselves fighting to expand their empire, which stretched from Turkey to Syria. Turns out the Hittites would send diseased rams and donkeys to the cities they wished to conquer, where they spread their "Hittite plague." The Hittites would then wait several years for their enemies to weaken, then invade and take everything. It was genius! Or it would've been, but the Hittites contracted the Hittite Plague, too. Other nasty forms of biological warfare would rear their ugly heads in the centuries ahead. Hannibal of Carthage launched pots full of venomous snakes onto the ships at Pergamon. The people of Hatra defended their fortress city against Roman invaders by hurling terra-cotta pots filled with scorpions. But perhaps the most revolting germ warfare occurred in 1346 with the Tartars' siege on the city of Kaffa. After the Tartar army was decimated by bubonic plague, they launched the corpses over the walls into the city, thinking the stench would demoralize their enemies. It did a lot more than that: it spread the plague. Kaffans fled the city, taking the Black Death with them. Many historians believe this was precisely how the plague got to Europe before spreading like wildfire and wiping out a full third of its population. Good going, Tartars. Way to fuck up a continent.

EASE OF USE: ★★★★ (viruses and scorpions are not safe to handle)
INVENTED BY: The Hittites
MADE INFAMOUS BY: Tartars; Hittites; Hannibal of Carthage; your own mother, who knowingly gave you chicken pox

THE FIRST TRUE SWORDS

When people talk about Bronze Age swords, they usually mean daggers. Most of the double-edged bladed weapons before 1500 BCE were too short to be considered longswords. That's because the bronze at that time couldn't hold its form when forged into anything longer than sixty centimeters. That all began to change when metallurgists discovered new methods of tempering bronze that allowed them to craft blades approaching three feet in length. (Now *that's* a fucking sword.) Swordsmen realized they could penetrate armor more easily by thrusting with a sharp point rather than slashing with a blade. So swordsmiths forged more versatile blades with both slashing and thrusting capability. These swords became even more legit with the inclusion of a pommel on the hilt. Not only did this prevent the warrior's hand from sliding off the grip, but now he could pistol-whip his enemy with the bottom of his sword if he didn't feel like killing him just yet. Despite the improved length, these Bronze Age longswords were still a distant third choice of weapon in most cultures, behind spears and javelins. The exception to this rule was the Chinese sword, or *jian*. The jian was considered the gentleman's weapon, as it required an educated swordsman to wield it. With two sharp edges *and* a thrusting point, it must have blown the thousands of ancient minds who struggled to master its potential. The Chinese would enroll in sword college just to unlock the infinite technique of the jian, and they would graduate with degrees in killing.

EASE OF USE: ★★★ (much steeper learning curve than one-sided "backsword" weapons)
DATE OF ORIGIN: 2000 BCE (Western Europe); 700 BCE (China)
TYPE OF DAMAGE: Cutting *and* stabbing!

WHO WANTS A PIECE OF ASSYRIA?!

You know the little angry guy who's always trying to pick fights with everyone in the bar? That's ancient Assyria. This Mesopotamian country just happened to be smack-dab in the middle of a prime piece of real estate that everybody wanted. The Assyrians had previously been pushed around by the Hittites. Mighty Babylon was to the south. The Scythians lurked to the north. And Assyria lay right in the middle with no natural boundaries. Like the guy in the bar, Assyria was bullied a lot as a child, and it had no choice but to become a mean son of a bitch. With the slightest provocation, Assyria would stab these neighboring countries in the neck with a pen while screaming, "Am I here to amuse you?!" And that pen just happened to be made of a new metal that most of the ancient world hadn't seen before . . . iron.

Assyria wasn't the first to figure out how to smelt iron. That honor likely belongs to the Hittites. But eventually, the Assyrians . . . ahem . . . *borrowed* the iron smelting technique from the Hittites, and proceeded to unseat them as the dominant power in the Middle East. Iron weapons were something of a novelty at this point, typically made out of meteorite iron—a naturally occurring alloy that fell out of the fucking sky. The material was scarce, however, since meteors don't land in your backyard every day. Assyria was the first to show up at a battle with an army that was completely strapped with iron, and the idea of an all-iron military had the entire ancient world shitting its tunics. They knew they had to get Assyria before Assyria got them.

With so many enemies, the Assyrians had to think outside the sarcophagus. They made damn sure their city walls were twice as fortified as everyone else's. But more importantly, they developed a system of siege warfare that made everyone else's walls look like they were made of straw.

So You Want to Seize a Fortified City

The easiest strategy when attempting to seize a city is the (1) *passive siege*. All you have to do is amass an army and have them camp outside the opposing city's walls to show those fuckers you mean business. This will keep any food supplies from reaching the enemy. With a little luck, your enemies will be starving to death within a year, and they'll wave the white flag.

Okay, so the passive siege takes a while. If you're feeling impatient, you could try (2) *mining*. First, you're going to have one of your men dig a trench, slightly closer to the city walls. When that's done, have your army run to this trench and take cover. Then have your digger make another trench, a little closer to the wall. Repeat this until you're close enough to dig underneath the city. But watch out—any adversary worth his salt is going to be listening for you, literally with his ear to the ground. He might try pumping noxious fumes into your mineshaft or filling the hole with water to drown your men.

If mining isn't your thing, you could always try (3) *going over the wall*. You could do this by ladder, or by building an embankment—a large earthen ramp leading to the top of the wall. And the top of the wall, as a rule, is going to be much thinner and weaker than the bottom. Walls of the Middle Eastern Bronze Age are almost guaranteed to be made of mud rather than rock, which can be hard to find in the middle of the desert. This means . . .

You can (4) *sap* (chip away) the wall pretty easily with a pick or crowbar. And once you've got a breach, it's all over but the crying.

You can also (5) *know a guy* inside the city. Sometimes the invading army would bribe someone from the other side to betray his own city and open the gate for them. Since people are dicks, this happened a lot more than you'd think.

BATTERING RAM

The easiest, most obvious way to breach a city's walls is to penetrate its weakest point. This is almost always the gate. The principle of the battering ram is simple: have several of your biggest dudes heave a large log at the gate as hard as they can. If they can gather enough momentum, the gate should come down like a Christmas tree in January. The Assyrians took this simple battering ram principle a step further by putting metal wheels under it and turning it into a siege *engine*. Then they put wicker canopies on top to provide protection for their troops as well as their ram. They covered the tip of the ram in iron, and suspended it from a system of ropes that allowed it to swing for even greater momentum. At times, the Assyrians used a large spear for the ram head, enabling it to chisel rather than bash. They even built an archery tower to provide protection for the men powering the ram. Simply put, the Assyrians invented the Batmobile of ancient Mesopotamia. But despite all its weapons, the battering ram usually needed a little more protection to do its job. That's where the siege tower came in.

EASE OF USE: ★★ (requires a ton of manpower)
USED WITH: Wicker or wooden canopy
PURPOSE: Knocking down walls and doors
PRECURSOR TO: Doorbell

SIEGE TOWER

This might be the crown jewel of crazy Assyrian warfare. Its purpose was two-fold: (1) To provide cover for the invading Assyrian infantry. Siege towers housed a number of archers and ranged weapons for this purpose. While these archers were keeping the defenders on the wall busy, the invading infantry would be able to approach the wall with ladders. In fact, the Assyrians were so badass they could climb these ladders while using both hands to fire arrows up the wall, meaning they were climbing the ladder with *no hands!* (2) The other function of a siege tower was to get close enough to the wall to support a bridge. When a siege tower had been wheeled close enough to the wall, the siegers could lower a gangplank, providing a walkway into the city. With the attacking archers covering them, the infantry would move across the gangplank and begin the melee fight atop the wall. All of this sounds easy, but there were obstacles. These towers were made of wood, and that meant the defending city would usually try to set them on fire. The Assyrians would have to be on constant guard for the fire attack, extinguishing these fires with ladles full of water. They also covered their siege engines in wet animal skins, making them less flammable, but probably more stinky. Imagine riding to war inside a giant wet dog.

DATE OF ORIGIN: 900 BCE

USED WITH: Battering ram; archers

USER REVIEWS: "Oh, shit! That house is attacking us!" —Town of Lachish, which the Assyrians seized in 701 BCE

SCALDING SUBSTANCES

By now you're probably thinking that seizing a fortress must be the easiest thing in the world. That's not exactly true. The people inside the city generally wouldn't just hand over their city. In fact, they would usually fight back pretty hard. They had one tactic at their disposal that was both simple and nasty: dumping scalding substances onto their invaders. Piping-hot cauldrons of liquid were poured onto invaders at the city walls, serving as one of the most effective deterrents to would-be castle stormers. Unless the invading army could tunnel in from a distance, they had no choice but to go near the walls. And that meant a pot of boiling-hot oil, water, resin, or even sand would always be waiting for them. Once dumped, these searing-hot substances could seep through any armor, including metal. Anyone who didn't go into shock from sheer pain would have to continue the siege with his flesh melting right off his bones. And if the invaders still weren't completely demoralized, quicklime was also poured into their faces, causing chemical burns and blindness. Aren't you glad you don't live in ancient Mesopotamia?

EASE OF USE: ★
USED WITH: Pots, cauldrons, and "murder holes" (holes built into castle walls specifically for scalding invaders)
PRECURSOR TO: Greek fire
MADE FAMOUS BY:
That kid from *Home Alone*

Chapter 3.

ANCIENT CHINESE SECRETS

1000–300 BCE

WESTERNERS have always been fascinated by the East. The people of the Orient have exotic spices. They write up and down instead of left to right. They fight with their feet and eat with sticks. They've also been pretty creative in the art of war, and I'm not just talking about the dreaded Chinese finger-cuffs. Asian civilizations were some of the most advanced of the ancient world, and the weapons they used were like nothing the West had ever seen.

STAFF

This simple wooden pole is one of the oldest weapons to come out of Asia. In fact, the Chinese call it the grandfather of all weapons, which explains why it eats dinner at four o'clock and always forgets your name. Like a lot of martial arts weapons, the staff started out as a farm tool. It was originally a *tenbin*, a pole used to carry buckets of water. But necessity is the mother of invention. You can imagine the scenario: Some farmhand was returning from the well with his newly fetched water, when he got jumped by highwaymen. He ditched the water buckets, spun his tenbin around and clocked his assailants. Or they murdered him, and took the tenbin idea for themselves. Either way, the *gun* (Chinese for "staff") was born on that day. Since then, this simple weapon has been celebrated by the Teenage Mutant Ninja Turtles, old kung fu movies, and Napoleon Dynamite. (If you're still having trouble picturing it, it's that stick they twirl around real fast.) It can be used to club, trip, parry, sweep, slash, poke, or pole-vault, and its length makes it ideal for mid- to long-distance combat. It can even be used to keep multiple assailants away. Though it had been used since antiquity, the staff wouldn't be recognized as a respectable weapon until the seventeenth century, with the development of the Japanese martial art *bojutsu*. The staff was no longer just a peasant weapon, and ancient Chinese hipsters would forever gripe about how they were into the staff before it was cool.

EVOLVED FROM: Tenbin (a tool for carrying water buckets)
PRECURSOR TO: Polearms
ALSO CALLED: Quarterstaff; *bo* (Japanese); "bo staff" (which redundantly translates to "staff staff")
USED FOR: Mid- and long-range melee fighting; limbo contests

CROSSBOW

Imagine that you're a Chinese emperor and some neighboring tribe of nomads is plotting to pillage your kingdom and rape your women. You need archers fast. But it takes years of training to become skilled enough to use a traditional vertical bow. Not only that, you need the upper-body strength of a chimpanzee to wield it. What's a Chinese emperor to do? Lucky for him, some ancient so-and-so invented the crossbow—a weapon that would revolutionize warfare in China (and later all of Europe). Sure, the crossbow is about as sleek and mobile as a hippopotamus. It also takes longer to load than a longbow. But you can load it anytime before the battle starts, saving you valuable seconds during combat. Furthermore, the crossbow's projectiles fly much faster than those of a vertical bow. Even though its bolts possess less mass than arrows, they're propelled by more draw weight (the force necessary to pull back the string). This means a faster and deadlier shot. But most importantly, it means the crossbow is *easy to use*. The string can be drawn with two arms, meaning that even the biggest weakling can load it. And it requires very little training, which ensures that this weapon can be used by the most lowly dirt-farming simpleton. The Chinese had lots of farmers, and they now had a weapon to arm them with. By the third century BCE, the Chinese were mass-producing these with bronze trigger mechanisms that made for a more reliable shot. The predominance of this weapon would ultimately allow the Qin army to conquer all competing Chinese kingdoms, uniting China in the biggest empire the ancient world had ever seen.

EASE OF USE: ★↗
USED WITH: Bolts, pellets (ammunition)
FUN FACT:
Modern-day prison inmates have been known to craft fully functioning crossbows from rolled-up newspaper

GE & JI

Few things were more terrifying for a warrior than fighting on foot while his enemies were on horseback. In almost every instance, the mounted combatant would squash the infantryman like a frog under truck tires. Eventually, the ancient Chinese came up with a way to level the playing field: they began arming their infantry with polearms. One of the originals was the *ge*, or "dagger-axe." As evident from its name, the ge was a dagger fixed to the end of a pole, and its primary purpose was to throw mounted enemies from their steeds and chariots. If it caught the neck, the dagger-axe could even rip clean through the throat and vertebrae to decapitate its victim. Over the years, Chinese engineers experimented with various angles of the blade. They discovered that if the angle was too great, the blade couldn't hook its target. If the angle was too small, the blade couldn't slash easily. They ultimately settled on a 100-degree angle—the perfect position for both hooking and slashing a horseman. (And you thought your protractor would never come in handy.) As if the ge wasn't enough of a killer, the Chinese added a spear to the tip—and yet another perpendicular blade to the end—forming the ji, the Swiss Army knife of ancient polearms. The ji could skewer, it could chop, it could hook, and most importantly, it could do it all from a distance. The foot soldiers of ancient China felt their balls grow three sizes. The prospect of facing down charging war chariots suddenly seemed a little less pants-shittingly scary.

DATE OF ORIGIN: 1800 BCE (ge), 1500 BCE (ji)
PRECURSOR TO: Medieval halberd
ADVANTAGES: Reach, especially important against mounted opponents
DISADVANTAGES: Can also be used by mounted opponents, in which case the opposing foot soldier is shit out of luck

Calling Bullshit
MYTHICAL HINDU WEAPONS

Ancient Indian history is a difficult riddle to solve. Not only is the information on this period very limited, but the records we do have typically come in the form of religious writings. And let's be honest: those can be less than reliable. The Indian epics the *Ramayana* and the *Mahabharata* contain extensive accounts of ancient Indian warfare. They mention real weapons like the *chakram* (see page 95), the mace, and the spear, but they also claim the ancient Indians had airplanes, invisibility shields, anti-aircraft missiles, and atomic weapons. Google "ancient India atomic bomb" and you'll see site after site claiming to have found evidence of irradiated dirt that proves the ancients of the Vedic period had mastered splitting the atom. All of the sites (some with perfectly legitimate names like *ufoevidence*) copy and paste the same text, and give no link or source for any of it. Any skeptic worth his or her salt should be, well . . . skeptical. No disrespect to anyone who believes this, but *come the fuck on*. Sure, I'd like to believe in *nagastra*, the divine weapon that summons thousands of snakes to rain from the sky. But a serious scientific publication like ours can't give credence to anything that doesn't have solid, empirical evidence supporting it. If I'm wrong, may nagastra strike me down.

EASE OF USE: ★★★★ (must be devout Hindu)
ADVANTAGES: Ability to destroy planets, dry up oceans, and make snakes rain from the sky
DISADVANTAGES: It's probably not real

WAR ELEPHANTS

One thing we do know the Indians had was elephants. Lots of them. And they were trained for warfare too, which was unlike anything the world's other armies had ever seen. The most immediate advantage of leading a herd of elephants into battle is the shock value. Not only is a squad of pachyderms going to turn your enemies' spines to jelly, it's also going to spook the hell out of their horses. It was not uncommon for an entire fleet of horses to flee the battle after smelling and hearing a hundred elephants coming over the hill. The other uses in combat are obvious: Elephants can stomp opposing infantry deep into the mud. So easily, in fact, that elephant stomps were prescribed by ancient India's Laws of Manu as a preferred method of capital punishment. Elephants also give a serious advantage to archers and javelineers, who can sit high atop the beast and rain a shitstorm of arrows onto the enemy without ever being touched. And if that's not enough of an advantage, you can equip your elephants' tusks with swords. (Seriously, what's going to beat an elephant with a sword?) There were even reports of Indian generals who affixed heavy metal balls to their elephant's tusks and trained the beasts to swing them like gigantic flails. The Asian elephants impressed Alexander the Great so much that he took a few back to Macedonia with him, and started the elephant revolution on the battlefields of Europe. Europeans began importing most of their elephants from Africa, and the demand was so great that they singlehandedly wiped out the entire species of North African forest elephants in just a few centuries. (Yay, white people!)

DATE OF ORIGIN: 1100 BCE
USED BY: India; China; Persia; Macedonia; circuses; and Hannibal of Carthage, who usually gets all the credit
ADVANTAGES: Strength, size, shock value
DISADVANTAGES: Elephants can go batshit and kill their allies if they're wounded

STEEL BOW

The composite bow is a solid weapon. It's relatively powerful, much more so than a single-material self bow. But—and this is no slight against any composite bow enthusiasts—it has problems with longevity. The enemy of the composite bow is moisture, and India certainly has plenty of that. And so the ancient Hindus were open to alternative materials. As one of the first—if not *the* first—countries to enter the age of steel, India had an obvious replacement for these composites. They began mining a substance known as *wootz*, an iron ore that would make some of the best steel for over a millennium. Carbon—as well as tungsten and other such alloying elements—acts a hardening agent between the steel particles, and this wootz stuff had just the right amount of it to create a perfectly hard, perfectly elastic, virtually indestructible steel weapon that could hold its edge for an eternity. Wootz bows were considerably more rigid than their composite bretheren, meaning they were also less powerful. But they were reliable and predictable, and could be stored away in munitions vaults without worry of decomposition. Like so many other people in history, the ancient Indians found themselves willing to sacrifice a little quality for a lot of convenience. They broke up with the unstable but good-looking composite bow and hitched themselves to the safe but boring steel bow, for better or worse. For the next few years, the steel bow became the ideal way to arm large groups of soldiers who would be fighting from a distance.

DATE OF ORIGIN: 300 BCE
MADE FAMOUS BY: That hillbilly chick from *The Hunger Games*
ADVANTAGES: Reliable, shiny, ornately adorned, can be used in the rain; perfectly safe and dependable
DISADVANTAGES: Less power; won't turn you on like your old composite bow

Chapter 4.

HEMLOCK
& SODOMY
(PARTY WITH THE GREEKS)

500–200 BCE

ANY PEOPLE consider ancient Greece the cradle of civilization. The Greeks produced countless philosophers. They were avid sailors. They participated in direct democracy. They practically invented art and literature. But more importantly, ancient Greece was the cradle of *good times*. The philosopher Epicurus encouraged his brethren to seek pleasure above all else. The Greeks responded by creating the drinking party, known as the *symposium*. They also ate four meals a day—all while lying on their sides. They could shred on the lute. They cranked out erotic sculptures like nobody's business. They even turned warfare into a party, getting wicked gay with each other in between battles—sometimes even *during* battles.

The Phalanx
Your Spear Is in My Aspis!

Just how gay was ancient Greece? This is a question scholars have pondered for centuries. For starters, the Greeks transformed the act of warfare into a group activity that involved hundreds of ripped, sweaty dudes piling on top of each other. The phalanx formation, as it was known, was a big, symmetrical square comprised of several rows of infantrymen. The soldiers, known as hoplites, locked arms and fought with their spears erect and their shields, or aspises, touching each other. Warfare would no longer be an individual sport. It was about moving as one massive, um, *unit*. The troops in the front of the phalanx attempted to penetrate the enemy lines with their shafts, while the troops in the back pushed them from behind. It was half war, and half orgy. A "war-gy," if you will, with the participants alternating between humping and stabbing. The front line of the phalanx was undoubtedly the place you didn't want to be. For one, you had to be in superhuman shape. Try pushing your couch around the living room for two minutes, and you'll get an idea of the type of conditioning they maintained. They also had to have balls of steel—if a man went to fight at the front of a phalanx, he knew there was a decent chance he wouldn't be returning to Athens. But as a consolation, he also knew he was going to be "Lucky Pierre" in the war-gy!

DORY

Phalanx formation didn't allow for the side-to-side slashing action of a saber. It demanded something with thrusting power. Thus, each warrior in the phalanx came with his own six-to-ten-foot spear—the *dory*—which was the most important weapon of ancient Mediterranean warfare. A phalanx clash typically began with both sides sprinting toward each other and colliding. It was not unusual for *all* of the spears in the front rows to break on this initial collision. But the brilliance of the dory lay in its other tip—which was also equipped with a butt spike, known as a lizard killer. This secondary spear tip served a few purposes: (1) You could use it when your spear broke and rendered the other tip useless. (2) You could plant it into the ground to brace yourself against the opposing army. (3) It was a nice way to finish off any enemies who might be lying wounded under your feet. (4) It made a good counterweight, allowing you to wield the spear with more stability. (5) You could fight dirty with it and skewer your enemy in the genitals—killing his lizard indeed. Exactly how the spears were thrust is still a hot topic of debate among losers with no girlfriends. The consensus seems to be that the soldiers in the front row wielded the spear in an overhead stab, while the rear hoplites held theirs upright until everyone in front of them had been killed. It was rare for a phalanx to lose that many people, though. Battles usually ended without large numbers of casualties, and the rear hoplites would pretend to be upset that they didn't see any action. Then they would go home and secretly cry to their wives/beards about how they almost got killed. Ah, the valor of war!

EASE OF USE: ★✦
USED BY:
Ancient Greek hoplites
FAMOUS VICTIMS: The Persians
at the Battle of Thermopylae
PRECURSOR TO: *Sarissa* (see page 59),
various polearms
USED WITH: Aspis; hot, sweaty
man-physique

SARISSA

Philip II, better known as Alexander the Great's father, must have had some serious issues with penis size. Under his rule, the Greeks began to phase out the dory in favor of an even *longer* spear—the *sarissa*. This new, massive pike was between twelve and eighteen feet in length, so large that it had to be gripped with both hands (tee-hee). This meant that the heavy aspis had to be discarded for a much smaller shield, but the sarissa proved to be worth the sacrifice. Hoplites had to undergo extensive training to use these new giant spears. They developed upper-body muscles they didn't know they had. By the time training was complete, these sarissa-wielding infantry could raise and lower their arms in unison, creating an intimidating *whoosh* from the wind they produced. These new arms were much longer than any weapon in use at the time, so naturally, the opposing armies had a rough time getting close to the new phalanxes. The sarissa was only effective within the phalanx, however. An individual soldier using it in the open was liable to be hacked to pieces by anyone who could get inside its reach. Another drawback was its unwieldiness. Even after an impressive training regimen, the infantry with sarissas took much longer to pivot, meaning they could often be outflanked and outmaneuvered, especially in uneven terrain. As the Greeks would learn the hard way, size isn't everything.

EASE OF USE: ★★★✦ (that shit is heavy!)
DATE OF ORIGIN: 359 BCE
ADVANTAGES: Long reach
DISADVANTAGES: Unwieldy; useless in individual combat; suggests obvious hang-ups with genitalia size

EARLY CATAPULTS

By the fourth century BCE, the people of the Greek colony of Syracuse, Sicily, were having a serious problem with Carthaginian invaders. The ruler of Syracuse, Dionysius the Elder, decided to amass a pool of artisans and engineers to develop weapons to defend the city, like a space program for ancient weapons. The result was the catapult. Not the medieval type with the scoop-shaped basket that we typically associate with the word. This was more of a large crossbow used as an antipersonnel device. Dionysius's crew used it to provide cover for their siege towers in taking the Carthaginian stronghold of Motya. In the years following, the Greeks would continue to expand the size of their catapults. They would discover that a bow could only be so large before becoming impractical. The Greeks would turn to a new catapult technology—the torsion spring—for their next wave of war machines. While the previous *gastraphetes* (literally "gut-bow") model propelled its projectile by pulling back a giant bowstring, the new torsion models—called ballistae—stored energy by twisting large coils of horsehair or animal sinew. When released, these coiled fibers would unwind and discharge the catapult's missile, which was now bigger and more powerful than ever before. Rather than firing puny wooden arrows, the torsion catapult could launch heavy stone balls. This meant it could take out walls, not just people. It could then use the pieces of the smashed wall as ammunition to smash more walls, like a self-feeding perpetual wall-smasher.

DATE OF ORIGIN: 400 BCE
BIRTHPLACE: Syracuse, Sicily
GUY WHO TOOK ALL THE CREDIT: Dionysius the Elder
PRECURSOR TO: Trebuchet (see page 114); onager (see page 71); futuristic death rays of tomorrow

ASPIS

The Greeks loved to talk about bravery in warfare. And it's easy to be brave when you're standing behind a massive shield like the aspis (or *hoplon*, as it's often known). This large bronze-plated oval was so impenetrable it's a wonder anyone ever died in the Greek phalanxes. In a way, we can thank the hoplon for the classical era. It kept the Greeks alive in battle, giving them more time to focus on art, philosophy, democracy, and pederasty. Without it, the phalanx wouldn't have been possible. It was enormous for its time—half the shield protected the wielder's left side, and half protected the man to his left. This, of course, meant that the unlucky bastards on the far right of the phalanx were left unprotected on their right sides. The aspis was also heavy, an estimated sixteen to eighteen pounds. Fortunately for the hoplites, the shield was designed to rest on the shoulder. Also fortunately, the aspis's mass meant that it served as a weapon in addition to a shield. It was not uncommon for a hoplite to swing the shield at his opponent after hacking with his sword (picture a one-two punch). A thrust with the aspis could knock a man down, and swinging it with the rim pointing out could break his jaw. But as amazing as the aspis was for the Greeks, in some sense, it ruined the excitement of battles. A well-shielded phalanx was probably a lot like watching a boxer with really good defensive skills. Sure, it's impressive, but who the hell wants to see that shit?

EASE OF USE: ★★
(considerable strength required)
ADVANTAGES: Keeps you alive
DISADVANTAGES: Makes warfare boring
USER REVIEWS: "I hit him right in the aspis for two hours. Nothing happened! We called it a tie and went home."

The Baddest Weapon of Antiquity
ARCHIMEDES' BRAIN

When most people hear the name Archimedes, they think of some principle they learned in science class. But know this: Archimedes was a genuine badass, and his brain was one of the most devastating weapons of the ancient world. Who was this mad genius of the Mediterranean? He was born in the Sicilian city of Syracuse, where he was under constant threat of siege by the greatest of armies—the Romans. Archimedes is best known for his math chops—he calculated pi to some ungodly digit. He wrote extensive explanations of levers and pulleys. He devised a formula to calculate density. While studying in Egypt, he developed a screw-shaped water pump that is used to this day. But, this being a book about weapons, we're going to focus on Archimedes' awe-inspiring machines of death. For starters: catapults. The old Greek war machines were crude and imprecise, but Archimedes' used his wicked math smarts to give them finer control. Archimedes' catapults could launch projectiles with a predictable flight pattern, allowing them to accurately hit targets that were hundreds of yards away. This was like witchcraft to the ignorant mouth-breathers of the time. He even made catapults in a variety of strengths and sizes. Archimedes designed holes in the walls of Syracuse to allow for the use of small hand-held ballistae called scorpions. He also surprised the hell out of the Roman navy with an invention called the Claw of Archimedes. As fantastical as it sounds, this pulley-powered crane would swing above the invading ships and drop a claw-like instrument into the water. The crane lifted the claw up, gripping the sides of the enemy ship and capsizing it. This terrified the Roman navy so much that they would tremble at the sight of any wooden beam extending over the water. Another alleged invention of Archimedes was the heat ray. According to the author Lucian, Archimedes set fire to invading ships by reflecting sunlight off hundreds of bronze shields. The validity of this account is shaky, especially since there is no mention of it before the second century CE, long after Archimedes' time. But hey, who's to say Archimedes' heat ray isn't alive in our hearts?

Chapter 5.

THE ROMANS: SICK FUCKS

200 BCE–300 CE

KAY. Before I get a ton of letters from all our ancient Roman readers, let me explain. It's not that the Romans contributed nothing to society. Remember the John Cleese bit, "What have the Romans ever done for us?" That pretty much sums it up. Many of their countless contributions to civic engineering are still with us today. Thanks to the Romans, mankind no longer had to shit in the street. For the first time ever, people had proper sewage systems to whisk away their waste. The Romans also gave everybody paved roads and water fountains. They were inventive, and what they didn't invent, they had the good sense to steal and claim as their own. They often improved these technologies. The Romans had some good qualities, but you have to admit they were *sick fucks*. They were such gluttons that they routinely vomited up their meals just so they could eat dinner all over again. They also got their rocks off watching slaves die in the coliseum. They turned crucifixion into a national pastime. And then there were the weapons they created . . .

GLADIUS

Sometime around the third century BCE, Rome found itself in conflict with . . . well, pretty much everybody. One of the many lands they did battle on was the Iberian peninsula (that's Spain and Portugal). While the Romans were busy taking a steaming crap all over their newly conquered land, they took note of the Spanish sword. The *Gladius Hispaniensis* caught the Romans' eyes. It was sleek, elegant, dual-edged with a savage point. It was reminiscent of the Greek *xiphos*, which had always been the red-headed stepchild of the Greek armies—a distant second choice behind the Greek spear. But the Romans saw potential in the gladius. They gave it a slightly "waisted" blade, meaning it bulged somewhat in the middle. The subtle distribution of weight toward the tip meant that it could hack like a mofo, almost as well as the nasty Spanish *falcata*. But while the falcata was a single-edged blade, the new Roman gladius had two razor sharp edges *and* a tip. The versatility was key. It was every bit as much a thrusting sword as a hacking weapon. And with a blade two feet in length, the gladius could be drawn by the right hand on the same side. This was important for the Roman legionary, who didn't want to accidentally maim a nearby ally by drawing across his body. This perfect combination of quality and convenience meant the gladius would rack up more kills than any other weapon in the entire ancient world. Gladius for the *vici*!

DATE OF ORIGIN: 200 BCE

BIRTHPLACE: ~~Spain~~ Rome

PRECURSOR TO: *Spatha*, a variant which was slightly longer to accommodate cavalry

FAMOUS VICTIMS: The Macedonians, who were chopped limb from limb by Roman gladii in the Battle of Pydna (168 BCE)

PILUM

This version of the javelin was one of the most important pieces in the ancient Roman arsenal. The Romans excelled at close-range combat, but they needed a way to get near enough to their enemies to use their deadly gladius blades. The *pilum* was a perfect way to close that distance. A sprinting legionary could launch a couple of these Roman javelins at his enemy while charging toward him. If the *pila* (plural for pilum) didn't kill the target, they would probably occupy him long enough for the Romans to get close and do the deed with their *gladii*. Pila weren't just deadly, they were annoying to anyone who happened to get hit with them. The iron tip of the weapon was intentionally untreated, causing it to be softer than usual. So as it pierced a shield or piece of armor, the Roman pilum would collapse and fuse with the enemy's equipment. Not only did this poor sap have a screaming Roman running toward him with a gladius in hand, he had to dislodge a crumpled iron javelin from his shield. The intentional crumpling also meant that the enemy wouldn't be able to throw the pilum back at the Romans. That had to be a plus, since dying from your own weapon can be a humiliating way to go.

RANGE: Twenty yards effectively

PRECURSOR TO: The *spiculum*, a later Roman javelin influenced by Germans

ALSO USED FOR: Picking up litter

PLUMBATA

Remember lawn darts? Those weighted missiles of death that were once a popular yard game like horseshoes? If you don't remember them, it's because they were taken off the market in 1988. The *plumbata* was an ancient Roman version of the lawn dart—a weighted projectile with a sharp point that was lobbed underhanded toward its target. And like the lawn dart, the plumbata killed its share of people. Not only that, it did it with ease. A typical Roman legionary could carry up to four plumbata inside his shield, making them easier to transport than a pilum. And since these darts were thrown underhanded, anyone could effortlessly granny-squat them into a crowded field of barbarians. The plumbata's power came from gravity—the higher it was thrown, the more force it had coming down. Like the pilum, the plumbata was used before the melee clash had begun, possibly as the armies were charging toward each other. An experienced legionary could toss all four of his plumbata into the air in rapid succession. This caused concern especially among enemies without helmets and shoulder armor. And even if the darts didn't take anyone out, they would distract the enemy long enough for the Romans to kill them with something else (see *gladius*, page 66).

EASE OF USE: ★
ALSO KNOWN AS: Lawn darts, Jarts
ADVANTAGE: Easy to carry and use
DISADVANTAGE: Difficult to aim, long trajectory = slow travel time
RECALLED BY: Roman Toy Safety Commission

CALTROP

Simple, damaging, and downright mean, the caltrop is a decidedly unsexy weapon. It's not fired from a ballista. It's not meant to hack limbs off. It doesn't even move. Yet, for thousands of years, the caltrop was an effective means of stopping infantry, cavalry, elephants, camels, and anything else with feet. It's basically the ancient version of those "severe tire damage" spikes, and it was strewn all over battlefields by the ancient Romans. It rests on any three of its spikes, and leaves the fourth one sticking up to impale the foot of an unlucky foe. In the case of galloping horses, this often resulted in falling, which could be fatal for the beast and its rider. Some versions were metal balls with spikes built into them. Some were two curved pieces of iron barb that were welded together at the centers. And some were basically just wooden planks with nails sticking out of them. But they all served the same purpose: to hobble the enemy and keep him from advancing. As is the case with a lot of weapons, the caltrop wasn't invented by the Romans, but it was made infamous by them. At the Battle of Nisibis, the Romans faced Parthian lancers riding dromedaries, a type of pretentious camel. The Roman infantry suffered significant casualties, but they quickly evened the score by crippling the dromedaries with a field of caltrops. With the Parthians' mobility hindered, the battle resulted in everyone's favorite outcome: a draw!

EASE OF USE: ❶

PRECURSOR TO: Landmines, "severe tire damage" spikes

USED BY: Persians, Greeks, Indians, Romans

USED AGAINST: Horses, elephants, camels, infantry with poor footwear

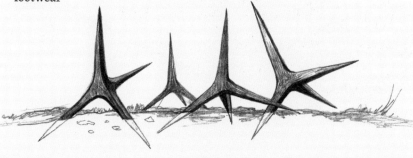

ONAGER

The ancient Roman onager had two things going for it: (1) It could chuck big pieces of rock through the air and take out ships, walls, cavalry, and chariots. (2) Its name literally means "wild ass," which is cool all by itself. The onager is probably what you think of when you hear the term *catapult*. Like the Greek machines before it, it's powered by torsion (coiled ropes or sinew). But unlike the ballista, which works somewhat like a crossbow, the onager had a single arm that sprung forward in a throwing motion. The arm was cranked back by turning giant gears on the sides. Modern reproductions of the onager indicate that this winding-up step was a grueling exercise that must have required several strong men. This leads us to the conclusion that the typical onager operators probably looked something like a BALCO-era Barry Bonds. Once the machine was sufficiently cocked, it was ready to be loaded with rocks, combustibles, dead animals, or whatever else the sick Roman fucks could come up with. When released, the machine made a violent kicking motion like a donkey—hence "wild ass"—and destroyed everything in the trajectory of its projectile. The onager team would then high-five each other, flex their enormous muscles, and take the lunch money of the other army.

EASE OF USE: ★★★ (requires muscle and mechanical savvy; high-maintenance)
ALSO KNOWN AS: Mangonel
PRECURSOR TO: Trebuchet (see page 114)
USED WITH: Rocks, incendiary projectiles, anything you want to get rid of

TRIDENT

Though this weapon was originally used by fishermen to spear multiple fish, the Romans adopted it for use in their gladiatorial bloodsport. Fighters in the Roman coliseum were typically given characters, much like your favorite professional wrestlers of today. One of the most popular was the *retiarius*, a mariner type who wielded a fisherman's net and trident. The gladiator would throw the weighted net to trap his opponent and follow up with a kill shot from the trident. When used on people, the weapon had to be modified somewhat. A typical mariner's trident might have all three teeth the same length. While this works fine on fish, it can actually make it more difficult to pierce the flesh (not to mention armor) of a human. Physics lesson: if the three tips hit simultaneously, the striking pressure is distributed over a larger area, making it harder to stab people. Thus, the middle prong of the gladiator's trident was often slightly longer than the other two. This gave the Roman trident more of a spear-like quality without sacrificing the pomp of costumed combat. The gladiators were happy that their equipment was more lethal, and spectators were happy that they got to see some folks get mirked with fishing equipment.

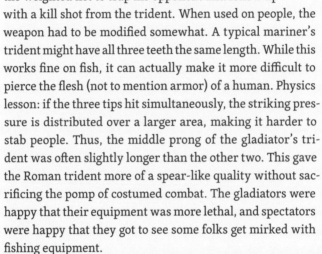

USED WITH: Net

LITERALLY MEANS: "Three teeth"

MADE FAMOUS BY: Poseidon, fishermen, Roman gladiators

OFTEN CONFUSED WITH: Pitchfork, a favorite of farmers and the Dark Lord Satan

FLAMING PIGS

If you're hoping this is a euphemism for something less horrifying, you might want to put the book down. Sometime in the first millennium BCE, the ancients discovered that war elephants were afraid of small animals that made strange noises (hence the longstanding belief that pachyderms are afraid of mice). Pigs were said to be particularly troubling, causing the elephants to become distressed at the slightest smell or oink of a nearby swine. Since the time of Alexander, Europeans knew that squealing pigs would frighten the tusks off attacking elephants. The first "war pigs" were sent into battle solely for the purpose of frightening elephants and breaking up enemy formations. Then, sometime around the third century BCE, the sick fucking Romans took it a step further: they coated the war pigs in oil and lit them on fire. Not only did this bring an incendiary weapon to the fight, it amplified the pigs' squealing and sent the opposing war elephants into an even bigger panic. Not to mention, it distracted the invaders with the tantalizing aroma of fried bacon. Though these incendiary pigs were probably an uncommon tactic, they are reported in the writings of Dionysius, Pliny the Elder, Aelian, and Polyaenus, whose name I believe means "more than one anus."

EASE OF USE: ★★★ɪ (burning animals are difficult to control)
MADE FAMOUS BY: Romans, Megarians, *Rome: Total War* video game
USED AGAINST: Elephants, most notably in the armies of Antigonus II Gonatas and Pyrrhus

I'VE BEEN CONDEMNED TO FIGHT IN THE COLISEUM.
Any Idea Who I Might Be Facing?

Good question. Here are a few of ancient Rome's popular gladiator characters:

Thraex Swordsman who carried a rectangular shield and a curved blade called the *sica*.

Sagittarius Mounted archer; had to be extremely accurate to avoid killing spectators in the stands.

Cestus Hand-to-hand pugilist who boxed with iron-studded hand wraps.

Hoplomachus Heavily armored gladiator modeled after the Greek hoplites. Armed with a spear and *gladius*.

Crupellarius Extremely heavily armored gladiator. Completely covered in iron. Not the most mobile fighter, but certainly the most impenetrable.

Laquearius Lightly armored combatant who used a lasso and short sword. Like an ancient Roman rodeo clown.

Scissores Used dual-tipped scissor-like blades, perhaps to trap an opponent's weapon.

Retiarius Agile, unarmored warrior with a weighted net and pitchfork.

Amazones Female gladiators, usually without helmet to show off the gender of the fighter. Used mainly for novelty and ridicule.

Andabata Fought blind, thanks to a helmet that blocked his vision. Also for ridicule.

Essedarius Drove Celtic war-chariot around the arena. Like a monster truck that crushed people instead of cars.

Dimachaerus Fought with two swords, one in each hand. Twice as deadly, but twice as vulnerable.

Eques Fought on horseback with lances, then would dismount and fight with a gladius.

Lions Kings of the jungle and the coliseum. Typically reserved for enemies of the state, including Jews, Christians, and other religious deviants.

Hoplomachus

Cruppellarius

Secutor

Myrmillo

Thracian

FALX

This heavy-hacking piece of weaponry was not Roman at all, but it certainly made a change in Roman warfare. The Dacians were a neighboring kingdom situated near the Black Sea (you know, where Communists used to go for vacation). Around the turn of the Common Era, they found themselves involved in numerous clashes with their Roman neighbors, who were all armed and armored to the gills. The Dacians happened to have substantial mineral wealth, and they mined enough iron to supply their army with an endless supply of falxes. The falx was a monstrous pole-arm resembling a scythe, with the sharp edge of the blade on the inside of its curve. It required two hands and all of a person's strength just to wield it. Unless the soldier had a third arm, there was no room for a shield or parrying weapon. With the falx, the idea was to come in swinging and take down as many enemies as possible before one of them had the chance to counterstrike. In this instance, offense really was the best defense. To the surprise of the Romans, the Dacian falx was capable of cutting right through their armor. With their tails between their legs, the Romans were forced to regroup. They fortified their helmets with a steel crossbar before attempting to conquer the Dacians and their mighty falx again.

DATE OF ORIGIN: First century CE
USED BY: Dacian warriors
PRECURSOR TO: Roman "siege hook"
ALSO AVAILABLE IN: Smaller size called the *sica*
ADVANTAGES: Excellent reach; vicious chopping power, could hack through Roman armor
DISADVANTAGES: Zero defense, as both hands are needed simply to control the falx

Chapter 6.

...AND YOU THOUGHT BUDDHISTS COULDN'T FIGHT

ASIA, 1–1000 CE

DURING THE FIRST millennium of the Common Era, the countries of Asia produced some seriously bizarre weapons. Martial arts were flourishing, and people all over the continent were turning their ordinary farm tools into skull-bashing, artery-severing, rib-cracking instruments of pain. It's often been said the Chinese could make a weapon out of anything. Rakes, scythes, brushes, pitchforks, cattle whips, walking canes, flutes, cymbals, and so help me God, even *coins* have all been modified for use as weapons. And to complicate matters, most of them have little or no written record of their use, forcing one to rely on legends of their origins rather than factual accounts. *Therefore, in lieu of facts, we are glad to provide you with the highly suspect information gathered from Chinese legend—marked by the symbol L.*

L = Legend

KWAN DAO

While some Chinese warriors were dedicating years of their lives to learn the ways of the double-edged *jian*, the *dao* presented a simpler alternative. This single-edged saber didn't offer all the moves of the jian, but it compensated with pure chopping power. The jian may have been the gentleman's weapon, but the dao could hack gentlemen to pieces, and it could do it with very little training. Still, some people saw room for improvement. "What if I need the hacking power of the dao but would also like to dismember my enemy from a distance?" Thus, the dao was affixed to a long handle, giving birth to the formidable *kwan dao*, one of the most iconic polearms of the East. Who's responsible for unleashing this beast of a backsword? General Guan Yu of the third century CE.[L] Yu was supposedly a gargantuan man, so large that he commissioned his blacksmiths to create this beast of a weapon just for his hands. Yu's kwan dao was named the Green Dragon Crescent Blade, and it allegedly tipped the scales at nearly a hundred pounds[L] (though most surviving specimens are more in the ten-to-twelve-pound range). As evidenced by its curved blade, 99.9 percent of the time the kwan dao was used for slashing. The back of the blade also contained a thumb-like notch that could trap an enemy's weapon, as well as several serrated teeth that were used for God knows what.

DATE OF ORIGIN: 200 CE (according to legend), 900 CE (according to most historians)
OTHER NAMES: *Guan dao, kuan tao, yan yue dao*
OTHER USES: Bottle opener for giants

L = Legend

MONK'S SPADE

This shovel-like weapon wasn't always a weapon. It was originally used by traveling monks to bury corpses they might find on their journey. Since it was the monks' religious obligation to bury corpses and not leave them to decompose on the side of the road, they often carried a spade to dig a grave and give the poor mofo a proper sendoff into the afterlife. Eventually, the monk's spade became something more than a trench-digger. The monks adapted it for self-defense, adding the crescent blade to the butt of the weapon. Not only could the monk's spade be used to bury old corpses—now it could be used to make *new* ones. Physically, the monk's spade is rich with Taoist symbolism. The five rings on the neck represent the five elements: earth, water, fire, metal, and wood. The dimensions of the weapon are said to symbolize various elements of the Buddhist afterlife, giving its victims a visual lesson on Hades before sending them there.

ALSO KNOWN AS: *Yue ya chan* (crescent moon spade)
USED BY: Taoist and Buddhist monks, particularly in Shaolin
EVOLVED FROM: *Fang bian chan* (earlier version without the crescent blade)
ADVANTAGES: Reach; can slash victim's throat from a distance
DISADVANTAGES: If Buddhist, wielder is required to bury his/her victims after slashing their throats

ROPE DART
& METEOR HAMMER

These two rope weapons are sometimes called *soft weapons*, though getting flogged with them probably doesn't feel like a hug from the Snuggle bear. In fact, the weights at the ends of them are capable of breaking skulls and sternums, making the rope dart and meteor hammer every bit as deadly as any other blunt force weapon. The meteor hammer is sort of the rope dart's bigger cousin. It's neither a meteor nor a hammer, but who has time to ponder the misnomer when you're being bludgeoned by the heavy metal balls on the ends of this thing? The rope dart was developed in the Warring States Period, circa 400 BCE. Its weight is smaller than that of the meteor hammer, but it's pointed, allowing it to slash and pierce as well as bludgeon. They're both swung in rapid circles—much like a sling or a bola—then flung at the enemy with tremendous speed. They can attack around shields. They can also be used to strangle an enemy or snatch weapons from his hand. And since they are "soft," these weapons can be folded and stowed anywhere on your person for convenience and secrecy. *However*, it should be noted that these were typically used as secondary weapons on the battlefield, drawn only if one's primary weapon had been lost or destroyed. It should also be noted that all "soft weapons" are difficult to use and should only be studied under the tutelage of a professional. If you break your face with a meteor hammer, don't come trying to sue me.

DATE OF ORIGIN: 400 BCE
PRECURSOR TO: Chain whip
ADVANTAGES: Easily concealed, circular movement ideal for striking around shields
DISADVANTAGES: Hard to master, can break user's face

CHAIN WHIP
(NINE-SECOND WHIP)

Believe it or not, not all Chinese people are proficient with a nine-section chain whip. I know what you're thinking: "Why the hell not?!" Well, like the other soft weapons, it takes years of training to wield a chain whip without maiming yourself. And you have to be in wicked good cardiovascular shape too, as the weapon must be kept in constant motion to be effective. The chain whip is constructed with a weighted point on the end, much like its rope predecessors. It's also spun in violent circles like its predecessors. But unlike its rope cousins, the chain whip is made entirely of metal, so the wielder is sure to feel his or her mistakes even more. A speeding chain whip will not only break your face, it can rip it clean off your skull, giving you added incentive to use it correctly. So the warning issued for the rope dart goes double for this weapon: *Do not use without professional training*. Once you've joined a proper dojo and are ready to begin training, don't go ripping the flags off your chain whip. They not only look pretty, they serve the practical purpose of balancing the weapon and making it easier to wield. Plus, they make a cool noise, not unlike a miniature helicopter. Now that I think about it, I'm going to play with one of these the first chance I get, professional training be damned.

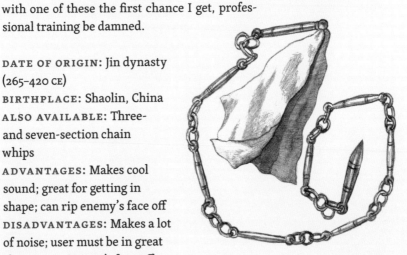

DATE OF ORIGIN: Jin dynasty (265–420 CE)

BIRTHPLACE: Shaolin, China

ALSO AVAILABLE: Three- and seven-section chain whips

ADVANTAGES: Makes cool sound; great for getting in shape; can rip enemy's face off

DISADVANTAGES: Makes a lot of noise; user must be in great shape; can rip user's face off

CHU-KO-NU
(REPEATING CROSSBOW)

Are you tired of constantly reloading your crossbow? Well, now there's a better way! As we discussed previously, crossbows were kick-ass. But the problem was always the same: after firing a shot, the wielder would have to stop in the middle of a fight, completely vulnerable as he fumbled to draw another bolt from his quiver. Then, hands trembling from adrenaline, he would have to place the bolt into its track, pull the drawstring back, and pull the trigger. And all of these steps had to be repeated after every single shot, making these crossbowmen sitting ducks on the battlefield. The Chinese, inventive bastards that they were, developed a solution: the *chu-ko-nu*, the world's first repeating crossbow. The cartridge on the top could hold arrows. With the pump of a lever, a new arrow was dropped from the cartridge after every shot, ensuring that the wielder was never left defenseless (for ten shots anyway). While traditional bows were all about placing carefully selected shots, the chu-ko-nu could rattle off about one shot every two seconds, raining down a shitstorm of indiscriminate crossbow fire that would scare the Fu Manchu right off the enemy. Though most of the shots wouldn't penetrate armor, one couldn't argue with the result—a thousand weak shots were more terrifying and more demoralizing than ten well-placed arrows from a composite bow. This power in quantity made the chu-ko-nu perfect for defending a city, scattering a charging battalion, or just impressing your friends on a Friday night.

DATE OF ORIGIN: 200 CE
INVENTED BY: Renowned battle strategist Zhuge Liang
DISADVANTAGES: Lack of power; won't penetrate armor; inaccurate
ADVANTAGES: Volume. Accurate enough to hit a horse.
ALSO AVAILABLE: Double-barrel chu-ko-nu (no shit!)

EMEI PIERCERS

Pretend you're an assassin. You're moving under cover of night, and your target just so happens to be surrounded by a protective moat. You're going to have to swim to get close, and your favorite halberd is going to seriously weigh you down in the water. There's only one weapon that's both effective and small enough to hold in your hands while swimming. The *emei* piercers, or twirling arrows of death, as I like to call them, were specifically designed for use in the water. Their streamlined shape causes minimal drag, allowing the assassin to swim normally, then leap from the water and strike his blow. The needles are often worn in pairs, with the user's middle finger inside the ring. The dagger pivots on the ring and can be spun very fast to baffle or confuse the enemy before striking. Once the arrow stops spinning, the warrior thrusts one of its tips into an enemy's pressure points or vital areas (e.g., temple, throat, heart, eyes, anything else he might need in a fight). Then the attacker disappears into the water and swims away like a bloodthirsty angelfish.

DATE OF ORIGIN:
900 CE (possibly)
BIRTHPLACE:
Mount Emei (Sichuan Province, China)
ALSO KNOWN AS: *Emeici*, emei daggers, *ba gua* needles
SIMILAR TO: Dark judge brushes, judge's pens

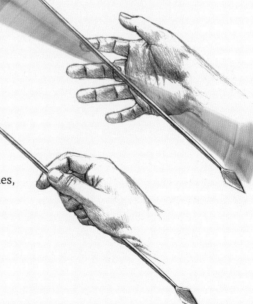

85

THREE-SECTION STAFF

This mean piece of lumber was invented by Zhao Kuangyin, before he became the first emperor of the Song dynasty. Zhao was a respected martial artist who worked as a bodyguard.[L] One day, while accompanying a wealthy client, his party was attacked by bandits.[L] Zhao cracked one of the robbers over the head with his staff, breaking the weapon clean in two.[L] Rather than buying a new staff like a normal person, he commissioned a blacksmith to connect the broken pieces with metal fittings and a chain.[L] He would later break one of the two remaining pieces again, forcing him to connect this third piece of wood with another chain.[LL] Some people just can't throw anything away. Like other flexible weapons, this is a difficult (and painful) one to master. Students typically learn by injuring themselves in training, causing them to modify their technique or break their hands. But the three-section staff is rewarding, allowing attacks from various ranges. It can be swung at full extension for a broad, sweeping attack that keeps multiple opponents away. It can be swung with two sections for a midrange assault. But the best use of this weapon may be its close-range function: the middle section crosses the user's abdomen while the other two are wielded in separate hands. Power is generated from the torso, with the staff whipping around the body like a Chinese hand drum. Perhaps Zhao Kuangyin was not as full of shit as he sounds.

DATE OF ORIGIN: 950-ish CE[L]

PRECURSOR TO: Nunchaku

INVENTED BY: Zhao Kuangyin, who was a dedicated husband, bodyguard, martial artist, Confucian philosopher, military officer, emperor, inventor of weapons, and god[L]

L = Legend

Calling Bullshit
THE FLYING GUILLOTINE

Introduced to the masses in the 1970s kung fu film *Master of the Flying Guillotine*, this weapon has captivated the imaginations of martial arts nerds for decades. In the film, a blind warrior wields a device that looks something like a beekeeper's mask. He throws it around the head of his victims, then pulls on a cord that causes a scissor-like blade in the mask to instantly decapitate his foe. Sure, the film is campy and in many ways terrible, but it forever changed the way fantasy geeks think about ranged weaponry. So what became of the flying guillotine? Why isn't everyone using it nowadays? Unfortunately, this beheading bad boy is a myth. Modern recreations have proven the flying guillotine was probably impossible to use in combat—or even in point-blank assassinations. Its range is poor. Its accuracy is suspect. Its construction is ridiculously convoluted. And the instant decapitation? Well, that's not so instant. And on the field of battle, anything less than instant is a ticket to your own graveyard. That's not to say the flying guillotine was never made and used to terrify people. I'm getting scared just writing about it. Now I'm starting to regret calling it a myth. Please don't kill me, flying guillotine.

Shaolin Butterfly Swords
The Buddha Fights Back

Like most monks, those of the ancient Shaolin temple were pretty religious. The tenets of their religion taught them the notion that murder was wrong. Even though the monks abhorred violence, they constantly found their temples being invaded, pillaged, and burned to the ground. This constant tragedy forced them to reexamine the whole "avoid killing or harming any living thing" deal. The Shaolin order developed an extensive system of martial arts, all the while insisting that its practitioners use only the minimum amount of force necessary to defend themselves. Sometimes this meant a simple wrist-lock on the aggressor; sometimes it meant planting a foot in his scrotum and sending his testes on a vacation to his abdominal cavity. Eventually, a vast array of quasi-lethal weapons were invented to suit this pacifist ethos, none more exemplary than the butterfly swords. These were peculiar blades. In fact, they were originally not really blades at all, but largely blunt weapons that were designed to disarm, parry, and defend—*not* to kill. The butterfly swords were typically wielded in pairs, one in each hand, twirled about the wielder's body so rapidly that they resembled butterfly wings (hence the name). The guard on the handle served as a knuckle-duster, for delivering nonlethal punches. The tip was completely dull, as was most of the edge. Only a three-inch section of the sword's edge was sharpened for cutting. This allowed the monks to disable an enemy by severing his tendons. Sure, the foe was humiliated, maimed, and crippled, but he usually lived to tell the rest of the world not to fuck with the Shaolin crew.

TIGER HEAD HOOK SWORDS

There aren't too many swords that look more menacing than the hook sword. And the hook sword backs up its fearsome reputation, too. The hook on its tip can grapple or snatch weapons from foes. The sharp point on the other end of the sword acts as a dagger (be careful not to cut your own hand off with this!). The crescent blade on the hand guard can block or slice at close range. The long edge of the weapon can hack right through a person's limbs. And the built-in kettle can brew up a hot cup of jasmine tea. Okay, so that last part isn't true, but that still leaves four useful tools packed into one wicked weapon. And if four blades weren't enough, the hook swords can be used in pairs, giving the wielder a total of eight weapons in his two little hands. Dual hook swords can also be attached and swung as one long blade, scaring the shit out of whomever has the misfortune to be standing across from it. Having said all this, the hook swords can be slightly inconvenient. Good luck finding scabbards that fit them. And good luck getting your wife to let you hang them on the wall.

EASE OF USE: ★★★★
(extensive training required just to keep from cutting your own hands off)

OTHER NAMES: *Gou, fu tao*

USED IN: Northern Shaolin schools

ADVANTAGES: Versatile and deadly; a Chinese Swiss Army knife that can kill you

DISADVANTAGES: Impossible to sheathe, really clutters up your backpack

KHANDA

If the ancient Chinese considered the *jian* to be the gentleman's sword, then the Indian *khanda* was surely the *man's* sword. Sturdy, heavy, and sometimes wielded with both hands, the khanda was the very essence of Indian manliness forged into one shining piece of wootz steel. Its blunt tip made it virtually impossible to thrust with, but that hardly seemed to matter. The khanda's two long, sharp edges were sometimes serrated for extra carnage. This, combined with the slight flare at the end of the blade, made the sword perfect for serious chopping. The Rajput warriors of ancient India swung this impressive man-blade over their heads in battle, daring anyone to step within reach. In the event that someone did get inside the khanda's effective range, the wielder could use the spike on the bottom of the hilt for stabbing in close quarters. No wonder the khanda was eventually incorporated in the religious symbols of the Sikh religion. Nothing says "I follow the message of God" like a broadsword that can send someone to meet Him.

EASE OF USE: ★★✦ (some strength required)
DATE OF ORIGIN: 300–600 CE
MADE FAMOUS BY: Rajput and Sikh warriors
ADVANTAGES: Major hacking power
DISADVANTAGES: Heavy, cumbersome; wielder must have deltoids the size of elephant nuts

KATAR

Ever wish there were a steel sword attached to your fist that would stab everything you punched? Of course you have. Fortunately, you can make that dream a reality. All you have to do is travel back in time to ancient India and pick up a *katar*—the Indian "punch dagger." The katar was a truly wonderful, strange, uniquely Indian weapon not found in any other part of the world. Apparently no other culture on Earth thought to design a punching sword. This is puzzling, too, when you see what the katar can do to light chain mail. Since the thrusts are performed by "punching" the katar directly toward its target, the wielder is able to generate much more power behind each stab. This allows for deeper wounds and easy penetration of light armor. The two bars on the sides of the grips offer protection, ensuring that the wielder's hand isn't chopped off by a counterattack. The katar was typically used by nobility, some of whom hunted tigers with the weapon just to prove their nutsack. Some of the later models had an added feature—squeeze the handles together, and two additional blades pop out from the sides of the weapon. There's no telling if these extra novelty blades would hold up in combat, but that's not really the point. The triple-bladed katar lets everyone know that you are thrice as rad as the average Rajput.

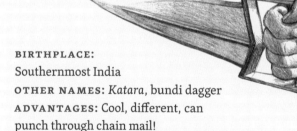

BIRTHPLACE:
Southernmost India
OTHER NAMES: *Katara*, bundi dagger
ADVANTAGES: Cool, different, can punch through chain mail!
DISADVANTAGES: Possibility of wrist injury
EVOLVED FROM: Knuckle duster (*vajra mushti*)
PRECURSOR TO: *Pata* (Indian gauntlet sword), Wolverine's adamantium claws

URUMI

The *urumi* is, without a doubt, one of the strangest and most interesting weapons ever devised by human beings. This exotic Indian blade is little more than a flimsy piece of band saw that the wielder swings around his body like a chain whip. Watching someone who's skilled with the urumi is a little like watching someone who's really good at playing five-finger fillet. You keep expecting the guy to seriously injure himself, but somehow he manages to keep pulling off the trick without losing a finger. That said, the urumi is still *extremely* dangerous to the user. It's one of the very last weapons taught in the Indian martial art of *kalaripayattu*, as the wielder must have great coordination and concentration just to keep from slicing his or her own face off while learning it. But if you ever need the edge of a straight razor combined with the flexibility of a bullwhip, and you've got years of free time to master the entire art of kalaripayattu, then the urumi might just be the weapon for you. Why did anyone ever bother with this exotic whip sword? The urumi's wide, sweeping attack protects the wielder's entire circumference, making it ideal for fending off multiple attackers. At the very least it makes them pause and wonder, "What the fuck is that thing?!" The urumi is ideal for women, as it relies on finesse and dexterity more than size or strength. At one point, the people of southern India preferred to use the urumi in settling personal disputes, since thrusting swords were not permitted in duels. And believe me—there's nothing like two angry, drunk Indians swinging band saws at each other outside the bar on Saturday night.

EASE OF USE: ★★★★★ (you'll shoot your eye out)
BIRTHPLACE: Southern India
OTHER NAMES: *Chuttuval* ("coiled sword"), *aara*
ADVANTAGES: Can fend off multiple attackers; can be worn as a belt
DISADVANTAGES: Extremely difficult to use; worthless against armor
USER REVIEWS: "Fuck! I just cut myself!"

HALADIE

Sometimes a warrior needs more than just one dagger. Sometimes he needs two daggers. And sometimes he needs those two daggers to be joined by the same handle with a knife coming out both sides of his fist. This is when he reaches for a *haladie*—the ancient "double-dagger" of the Rajputs. Indo-Persian daggers came in a variety of curves, waves, recurves, undulations, and bifurcations, and the double-bladed haladie has twice as many. The dual blade accomplishes two things: (1) it looks twice as badass, and (2) it gives the wielder twice as much stabbing potential. After a forward stab with one side of the haladie, the warrior can thrust the other blade with a backhand—and without having to reposition the weapon as one would with a traditional dagger. This allows the warrior to become a perpetual stabbing machine without ever having to stop and adjust. And as if that weren't awesome enough, some haladies are even crafted with a third blade protruding from the grip, making it three times as awesome! But why stop there? One can only pray for the day when a fifty-bladed haladie is invented in India. It wouldn't even need a handle— just kick it with your foot toward the enemy!

USED IN: India, Persia, Sudan, and everywhere in between

PRECURSOR TO: *Madu* (see page 205), fakir's crutch (see page 202), Darth Maul's double light saber

ALSO AVAILABLE: Triple-bladed haladie, single-bladed *bich'hwa* dagger

CHAKRAM

Frisbee, no matter how "ultimate," is a tedious game. It's slow and pointless, the disc takes forever to land, and it never goes where you want it to. The Sikhs and Rajputs, on the other hand, knew of a surefire way to make the Frisbee exciting. These longtime defenders of India made one of the most interesting projectile weapons in the history of warfare—a sharp metal ring of death called the *chakram*. It was less like a disc and more like a halo (picture those discs from *TRON*, only ancienter and realer), and it was an essential part of the arsenals of certain Indian warriors for many centuries. While it's doubtful the chakram could pack the wallop of a steel bow or an atlatl, we know it struck terror in the hearts of many warriors attempting to take northern India. Chakrams were easier to wield from horseback than the oversized Indian bows, and they could be worn on the arms and concealed in turbans—in large numbers, at that. They could also be thrown several at a time for a badass shotgun-style discus attack. If a chakram was made properly, it could fly without sound. And possibly land in some poor bastard's jugular before he ever knew it was coming. See? That's way better than Frisbee. Just don't throw it to your dog on the beach.

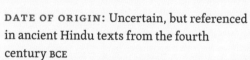

DATE OF ORIGIN: Uncertain, but referenced in ancient Hindu texts from the fourth century BCE

ALSO KNOWN AS: War quoit

ADVANTAGES: Unique, fashionable (can be worn as an accessory)

DISADVANTAGES: Dogs always running off with them

PRECURSOR TO: Aerobie

MADE FAMOUS BY: Vishnu, Xena Warrior Princess

Think You're Tough?
THE RAJPUTS WOULD TOTALLY BEAT YOUR ASS

In the pantheon of toughest all-time warriors, the Indian Rajputs are often overlooked. They're not quite as famous as the samurai or the Roman gladiators, not as iconic as the Spartan hoplites, and not as well-traveled as the Mongols. But believe this: the ancient Rajputs could hold their own against 99 percent of history's baddest fighters. From about the sixth century onward, the Rajputs defended the borders of northwestern India against countless Muslim invaders who wanted to claim India's fertile farmland for their own. From atop horseback, the Rajputs patrolled the vast Himalayan terrain with the swagger of Bengal tigers in heat. In later centuries, they were so ballsy they frowned upon firearms, which were clearly for cowards. The Rajputs' primary weapon was the khanda, though they were also proficient with the *tulwar* (see scimitar, page 113), lance, bow, *katar*, *haladie*, battle-axe, and to a much lesser extent, the chakram and *aara* (*urumi*, see page 92). But even more impressive than their balls and their weapon skill was their tenacity. The Rajputs were the descendents of kings, and their pride in their royal ancestry forbid them from allowing foreigners to have dominion over them. In the unlikely event that the Rajputs were losing a fight, they would throw themselves into certain death on the battlefield to avoid the shame of surrendering (especially to non-Hindus). And it was not uncommon for their wives and children to follow them into the afterlife by burning themselves alive. This legendary tenacity so impressed the British that the Rajputs were labeled a martial race—meaning they could rumble without giving a fuck.

Chapter 7.

BARBARIANS, BYZANTINES & BEOWULF

EUROPE'S DARK AGES

400–1300 CE

A S WE SAW in Chapter 3, the Romans were a massive pain in the ass for anyone living within a thousand miles of the Italian peninsula. But eventually, little by little, the Roman army was spread too thin. They enlisted the help of neighboring barbarians, and before they knew it, the Roman army was full of stammering savages who didn't give two shits about the empire. Rome fell. Barbarians ran roughshod over the European countryside, raping and pillaging as they pleased. Chaos ensued, punk rock was born, and a new cast of wacky tyrants made their way onto the world stage. These new guys would make the Romans look like Sunday school teachers.

A DATE WITH ATTILA
Having Dinner with "The Scourge of God"

Congratulations! You've been invited to dinner with Attila the Hun. Here are a few things you should know first:

The scar on his cheek is a Hun thing. They cut the cheeks of their children at a very young age. It's not as cruel as it sounds, though. They're just preparing them for the pain of life on the open steppe. Hun parents do other mean things to toughen up their kids, like naming them Attila.

Don't bring up his brother Bleda the Hun. He ruled for a brief time before Attila. He died in a suspicious hunting accident, possibly at the hands of Attila. It's a touchy subject, and it's best to avoid it.

Attila may be fabulously wealthy, but he doesn't *use* any of his valuables. He drinks from wooden cups, sits on a wooden throne, and lives in a wooden house, while all that gold just sits in his coffers. Go figure. But he insists that his guests eat from the fancy dishes. So don't be rude—use the silver.

Whatever you do, don't make the joke, "So, you must be really *Hungary*." He's heard it. And he hates it.

Attila is a tad arrogant. He believes his power is sent from above. Legend has it he possesses the sword of the war god Mars, so there's that. And his nickname "The Scourge of God" speaks volumes about his ego.

Don't count on him picking up the check. In fact, he might demand that you pay *him* in gold. It's best that you do it. Otherwise he'll be whipping out the aforementioned Sword of Mars, and your innards will be splattered all over the dessert cart. Please, just pay the man.

HUN HORSES

The only thing tougher than the Huns was their horses. Attila and his crew pillaged everything between China and France with the help of this animal, which they began riding before they could walk. The only reason we're talking about horses at all in this book is because the steeds of the Huns were a weapon unto themselves. Faster than anything God or man had created up to this point (except for the cheetah, which was too small and ornery to ride), the Hun horse was a snorting beast from hell that was reviled by the more "civilized" Romans. The Hunnic horse was typically leaner than its Roman counterpart. It was butt-ugly, with bulging eyes and long, tangled hair—a nightmare of sinew and protruding bones. It was kept in the pasture year-round without shelter, unlike the candy-ass ponies of the Romans, which enjoyed luxuries like stables and veterinary care. Because of this lack of pampering, the Hunnic horse had an incredibly hardy constitution. It could gallop for hundreds of miles without getting tired or sick. Once enemies were spotted, the Hun horses would encircle them while their riders unleashed a hellish storm of bone-tipped arrows from their composite bows. When every last enemy lay dead on the ground, the Hun horses would then gallop off to conquer some other country thousands of miles away. They were even responsible for giving the Huns milk along the way. What the fuck have your pets done today?

EASE OF USE:
★★★ (riding lessons required)
PRECURSOR TO:
Mongolian horse
USED WITH: Hunnic bows; whips instead of spurs
FAMOUS VICTIMS: Europe, which it galloped across at breakneck speeds

FRANCISCA (THROWING AXE)

The Franks didn't invent the axe. Nor did they invent the throwing axe. But they may have been the first to put it to regular use as a standard part of their military arsenal. In fact, they used it so much and so well that people stopped calling it a throwing axe and named it after the Franks themselves. The *francisca* may not have killed as many people as a bow and arrow, but its effectiveness was unquestionable. It was used in much the same way as the Roman pilum and plumbata. Once the Frankish forces were within forty feet of the opposing army, they would hurl their axes—most likely in a high, overhead arch—and cause sudden panic in their adversaries. The enemy's shields would go up to block the hail storm of axe blades raining down on them. Even if the axe didn't land on its edge, the head was still heavy enough to shatter a wooden shield with blunt force alone. And even the axes that missed were dangerous, as they would usually bounce off the ground in unpredictable directions. The enemy would scatter in fear of catching a francisca in the taint. All this chaos would give the Franks plenty of time to move in and run their opponents through with spears or club them to death with stale baguettes.

DATE OF ORIGIN: 400 CE

PRECURSOR TO: Dane axe; medieval hurlbat

ADVANTAGES: Concealable; can shatter wooden shields; can chop firewood; huge psychological effect on enemies

DISADVANTAGES: Has less range than a bow; must be within forty feet to use

MADE FAMOUS BY:
The French; circus performers; Dwarven warriors with a dexterity higher than 12

THE TOP 10 MYTHOLOGICAL WEAPONS OF ALL ERAS

The early Dark Ages were home to both Beowulf and King Arthur. So what better place to compile our top ten mythological weapons of every era?

10 Ame-No-Nuhoko Why not kick off our list with the Shinto weapon that began all life on Earth? Used by the gods Izanagi and Izanami, this bejeweled *naginata* (see page 130) was dipped into the oceans to make the first solid land on earth. Thanks for making the continents, Japan.

9 Narsil Straight from the mind of J. R. R. Tolkien, this bad boy was broken in two when Elendil used it to whack the Dark Lord Sauron. Many Tolkien books later, the Narsil was glued back together by sexy elves and renamed Andúril, which means "Viggo Mortensen's sword."

8 Ruyi Jingu Bang In the Chinese novel *Journey to the West*, the Monkey King is a rebellious creature who makes himself immortal through Taoist practices. He gains unlimited strength and is ultimately given a magical iron rod known as Ruyi Jingu Bang. This rod has the power to blow up into a monstrous eight-ton staff. It can also multiply and fight on its own. But perhaps most importantly, it can shrink down to the size of a sewing needle and rest behind the Monkey King's ear. Convenience is everything.

7 Zeus' Thunderbolt Zeus was the most powerful god in the Greek pantheon, and the thunderbolt was his weapon of choice. It was first given to him by a Cyclops (how fucking metal is that?). From high atop Mount Olympus, Zeus could hurl his bolts at any living thing that displeased him.

6 Mjölnir Thor's hammer, Mjölnir, was capable of much more than crushing his enemies. It was powerful enough to level mountains. He could also throw it through the air and hit any target, no matter how far away. Even more awesomely, after the hammer had flattened its victim into lingonberry pancakes, it would return to Thor's hand.

5 The Sudarshana Chakra This spinning discus was more than a steel *chakram*. It was Lord Vishnu's weapon of ultimate destruction. Created by Shiva, the *chakra* was given to Vishnu to kill demons that were tormenting the gods of Hinduland. The chakra was covered in two rows of sharp points, which rotated like saw blades. The weapon wasn't thrown with the hand but by the power of the mind. Once launched, it would hunt down the enemy and destroy him physically and spiritually. Think about this the next time you want to start shit with a Hindu deity.

4 Excalibur Often confused with the Sword in the Stone (a completely different sword), Excalibur was the blade given to King Arthur by the Lady of the Lake. Not only did this make him the sovereign ruler of Britain, but it made him unkillable, which is generally a good quality to have.

3 Light Saber If you don't know what this is, you probably live underwater. The light saber takes the bronze in our mythological weapons competition.

2 Gáe Bulg No, it's not pronounced "gay bulge," and it's not remotely pornographic. But it's pretty cool anyway. Gáe Bulg is the spear of the legendary Celtic warrior Cúchulainn. This mythical weapon is ranked number two for its originality: it was thrown with the toes. Once the spear had pierced the flesh, its barbs fanned out, making it impossible to remove. But most importantly, it was used by Cúchulainn to kill his best friend Ferdiad by piercing him through the anus. Okay, so maybe that's a little pornographic.

1 Zulfiqar This bifurcated menace is number one on our list for several reasons. It was sent from heaven to Muhammad (photo not available), who passed it along to his warrior/cousin Ali. With his new Zulfiqar, Ali slayed a Meccan soldier who possessed the strength of a thousand men. Many Muslims believe the Zulfiqar killed more people than any weapon in history. As if that weren't enough for it to claim the top spot, its name literally means "cleaver of the spine." Winner, winner, shawarma dinner!

GREEK FIRE

A substance whose name hardly does it justice, Greek fire was bad stuff that could ruin anyone's day. A better name might have been "Satan's shit," since that's exactly what its victims thought they were seeing when they were engulfed in this liquid hellfire. A combustible liquid that was squirted through large tubes, Greek fire is often thought of as the ancient world's napalm. It clung to its target and burned until it was spent, and you couldn't extinguish it with water. Its exact ingredients were a closely guarded secret, still unknown to this day, though most scholars think it probably involved petroleum, sulfur, pitch, and/or potassium nitrate. The first documented use of Greek fire was in 672 CE at the walls of Constantinople, the capital of the Byzantines. With an armada of Arab ships on their way to claim the city for Allah, a bright young architect named Kallinikos whipped up a batch of Greek fire, which he allegedly invented on the spot. With the help of this ancient napalm, the Byzantines sent the Arab fleet up in flames and thwarted not one but *two* Muslim invasions (before eventually losing the city to the Muslims in 1453). Later variations of the weapon were launched in clay grenades, giving the Greek fire even more range and allowing the Byzantines to incinerate every living thing within a three-hundred-yard radius of their city. Good times.

DATE OF ORIGIN: 672 CE
TYPE OF DAMAGE: Incendiary
PRECURSOR TO: Napalm
FAMOUS VICTIMS: The Arab navy

DANE AXE

As everyone knows, the Vikings were big mofos who needed big weapons. The broad axe, or Dane axe, as it's more commonly known, was exactly that—a big, heavy skull-cleaver that had to be wielded with both arms. This wasn't the primary weapon of the Vikings. (That would've been the sword and spear, which we've already covered ad nauseam.) It was, however, one of their coolest and most emblematic armaments. The Vikings began using axes out of necessity. The axe was a plentiful weapon that everyone had lying around the house, so it soon became co-opted for warfare. As the axes became adapted more for splitting skulls than firewood, their blades started to become thinner. By the tenth century, the bona fide Dane axe was born—a sharp, thin blade able to chop right through helmet and skull. The wielder could even use it to hook an opponent, pull his legs out from under him, or disarm him. It was, however, a somewhat unwieldy weapon. It lacked the speed and agility of a sword, and its wielder was completely unprotected, since he didn't have a free hand for a shield. This meant the Viking axeman was not usually the first line of defense. He would hang back, and just when the enemy's defenses were down, the axeman would swoop in and plant his Dane axe right in his opponent's cerebral cortex. Then the Viking axeman would retreat to the mead hall for a night of merriment and epic poetry recitals.

DATE OF ORIGIN: 900 CE
USED BY: Vikings; Saxons; Duke of Normandy's bodyguards
ADVANTAGES: Power; can cleave through a helmet; surprisingly versatile; easy to find
DISADVANTAGES: Slow; momentum is a bitch; easily outmaneuvered by a skilled swordsman; *zero* protection

JESUS VS. MUHAMMAD: WEAPONRY OF THE CRUSADES

They don't call it the Dark Ages for nothing. Ignorance reigned supreme, and religious fervor held sway in lieu of intellectual curiosity, which wouldn't come to Europe for another few centuries. In many ways, *Homo sapiens* had taken a big step back. Instead of using the sewage systems of the Romans, man now crapped in a bucket and tossed his waste right out the window. People were—literally *and* figuratively—ankle-deep in shit. Luckily, the Pope had a solution. Instead of Europeans walking around in their own feces and fighting each other, how about they get a posse together and go kick some Muslim ass? It sounded way better than sitting at home with all that excrement. And so it was that white Christians from all across Europe began the migration to reclaim the holy city of Jerusalem from the Saracens (the crusader term for all Muslims). Knights in shiny plate armor prepared to fight side-by-side with toothless hicks from the sheep farms, all hoping that God would give them extra heaven points for fighting the Holy War. On paper, it was a solid plan. In actuality, the Christians were about to embark on the suckiest vacation in history.

FLANGED MACE

The Muslim armies found themselves facing a European foe that heavily out-armored them. This was partly due to the scarcity of iron in the Islamic countries and partly due to the Muslims knowing not to wear heavily padded armor in the hot fucking desert. Regardless, they still had to contend with a European soldier who was covered in thick, padded chain mail. Slashing weapons like the backsword weren't going to penetrate this metallic membrane. Luckily for the Muslims, the mace had been undergoing a facelift over the centuries. It now featured deep flanges—or ribs—that could tear up heavy infidel shields and armor like they were junk mail. It quickly became one of the chief weapons of the Islamic infantry, who broke many an Anglo-Saxon skull with their new flanged maces. This made such an impression on the Europeans that they decided to use this ribbed head-splitter on each other as soon as they got back home.

EASE OF USE: ★★
DATE OF ORIGIN: 1100 CE
BIRTHPLACE: Persia, Russia, Byzantine Empire
ADVANTAGES: Can bust up armor like nobody's business
DISADVANTAGES: Somewhat heavy; not as quick as a longsword
GIVES EDGE TO: Muhammad

LANCE

Everyone knows an infantryman with a spear can cause a lot of damage. If that foot soldier is properly trained and conditioned, his spear can skewer enemy torsos like a toothpick through a club sandwich. Now take that same weapon, bulk it up a bit, and put it in the hands of a horseman. That toothpick suddenly becomes much more powerful. Why? Because the horse is supplying the momentum—packing far more force than the thrust of an infantry spear. The ape on top of the horse has only to hold the lance in a "couched" position (locked under the arm) and aim it at its target. You would think this would be a cakewalk for the knight, but you'd be wrong. Lances were massive, and it could be a physical feat just to keep them up (insert dick joke here). Nonetheless, the lance would become one of the chief weapons of the Crusaders, who often found themselves attempting to run down mounted archers in Muslim lands. Exciting as it was, jousting eventually devolved into the tournaments of the later Middle Ages, which involved blunted lances that couldn't puncture Saran Wrap. Boo, safety!

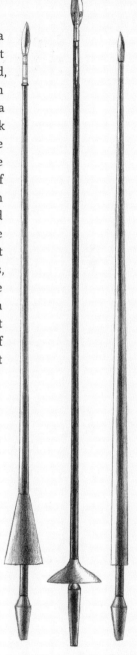

EASE OF USE: ★★★ (even though the horse does all the work, holding a lance steady is much harder than it looks)

DATE OF ORIGIN: 300 BCE

BIRTHPLACE: Ancient Iran

EVOLVED FROM: Spear

USED BY: Byzantine cavalry, Medieval European cavalry

OTHER NAMES: Pike (when used by infantry), "pointy horsey stick"

FUN FACT: In romantic literature, jousting represented sexual intercourse. Hot!

GIVES EDGE TO: Jesus

LONGSWORD

Though not widely used until the end of the Crusades, the longsword became a true symbol of the movement to reclaim the Holy Land. The knights discovered that if they held the sword with the handle pointing up, it made a swell cross. But in addition to the convenient symbolism, the longsword was also a pretty effective weapon. As its name indicates, it had a substantial reach advantage over the pathetically named "short" sword, and it put on the length without becoming noticeably heavier. Though it had a simple design, the European longsword was a quick and graceful weapon, moving with speed and versatility, able to cut, thrust, stab, and parry circles around its heathen opponents. One can only assume the enemy was so dazzled by the cross-shaped longsword that he abandoned his false prophet and accepted Jesus as his savior. Over time, the longsword became even sleeker and more thrustable. Grooves called *fullers* were forged into the blade, making it even lighter. A sophisticated system of fencing was codified in the fourteenth century, and the sword was given a sharper tip to penetrate armor more easily. It then acquired the nickname "bastard sword." This was partly because it was something in between a two-handed sword and a one-handed sword, and partly because its sword parents weren't married.

EASE OF USE: ★★★↗ (Though light and manageable, the wielder must learn sophisticated techniques. Must also be Christian.)
DATE OF ORIGIN: 1250 CE
EVOLVED FROM: Roman *gladius*, Viking sword
GIVES EDGE TO: Jesus

SCIMITAR

I know, I know. It's a stereotype—Arabs riding around the desert with curvy swords trying to hack up sweaty, sunburned white people who obviously don't belong there. But like it or not, by the end of the Crusades the Muslim armies were beginning to flirt with the scimitar—otherwise known as "that weird Middle Eastern sword they use in *Aladdin*." Mind you, *scimitar* is an umbrella term that covers curved swords from all over Central Asia and the Middle East. In Persia, it was known as the *shamshir*. In India, it was *tulwar*. In Turkey, it was the *kilij*. All of them featured a curved blade (sometimes *dramatically* curved), and all of them freaked the fuck out of Westerners. The curved blade would become a symbol of the differences between the two armies of the Crusades. If the European longsword was the cross, then the scimitar might be the Islamic crescent. The scimitar was practical too, especially from horseback. Thanks to the curve of the blade, a mounted warrior could pull the sword through his victim more easily without it getting stuck, whereas the straight longsword tended to stick in the wound, increasing its chances of being dropped in battle. This is what made the scimitar the sultan of slashing in the weapon world.

DATE OF ORIGIN: 900 CE

BIRTHPLACE: Persia or Central Asia

REGIONAL VARIATIONS: Shamshir (Persia), kilij (Turkey), tulwar (western India/Pakistan), *saif* (Arabia)

MADE FAMOUS BY: Arab stereotypes

ADVANTAGES: Major slashing power, especially from horseback; won't get stuck in its victim; if you rub it, a genie has to grant you wishes

DISADVANTAGES: Not as versatile as a longsword; the genie is an asshole who always gives you exactly what you do not want

GIVES EDGE TO: Muhammad

TREBUCHET

As fun as it probably was for Christians and Muslims to fight each other with melee weapons, the Crusades were really all about the big guns. The Christians built catapults, launched large chunks of rock at a Muslim city, and conquered it. Then the Muslims built their own catapults, hurled stuff back at the city, and reconquered it. It was a vicious cycle, and it was about to get even more vicious with the advent of the biggest rock-hurler of all: the counterweight trebuchet. Trebuchets were not new. They had been around since the fourth or fifth century BCE, when they were developed in China. But these old "traction trebuchets" required manpower to launch their artillery. They were decidedly lame, and will not be discussed further in this book. But once the trebuchet arrived in Arab and Byzantine lands, things got high-tech. A counterweight was added, providing a little more force for the launching mechanism. Then in the thirteenth century, the French blew everyone's minds with the world's first true counterweight (or "counterpoise") trebuchet. This machine didn't require a dozen sweaty dudes pulling on ropes to fire it. All it needed was gravity. The trebuchet could launch several hundred pounds of rocks at fortified structures, tearing through them like a Frenchman tears through frog legs. Counterweight trebuchets would get increasingly powerful, eventually able to launch a full *ton* of artillery at once. (That's the equivalent of a Honda Civic flying at your castle.) The counterweight trebuchet had another advantage over old engines like the onager: It was easy to maintain. Torsion engines had to be fit together with precision-crafted gears and fittings, while the trebuchet was much more apt to be constructed on the fly. All you needed was a wooden lever, a sling, a counterweight, and a Honda Civic, and *boom*—so long, city walls.

BIRTHPLACE: China, fifth century BCE (lame version); France, thirteenth century CE (awesome version)
USED UNTIL: Fifteenth century, when it was made obsolete by firearms
EVOLVED FROM: Mangonel, onager
FAMOUS VICTIMS: Dover Castle, which was pounded by

French trebuchets; the Song dynasty, which was defeated by Mongol trebuchets at the battle of Xiangyang

ADVANTAGES: Relatively easy to build; very powerful; can be used to seize sacred lands

DISADVANTAGES: Annihilates sacred lands in the process

GIVES EDGE TO: Jesus *and* Muhammad

OTHER KEY WEAPONS: Crossbow (Jesus), composite bow (Muhammad)

HOME FIELD ADVANTAGE: Muhammad. (Come on, you've seen what happens to white people in the sun.)

WINNER: Muhammad! The Muslims celebrate a decisive victory over the Christians, who have surely learned never to invade the Middle East ever again. And it just so happens that in the final battles of the Crusades, the Saracens get a little help from a Chinese invention called gunpowder . . .

Chapter 8.

ASIA BLOWS UP

CHINA & MONGOLIA, 1000–1300 CE

BEING ASIAN in the Middle Ages was probably both thrilling and terrifying. While the West was concerned with recapturing Jesus' manger, the Chinese were making serious advancements in the science of blowing shit up. Sometime around the ninth or tenth century ce, a team of Chinese alchemists was attempting to find an elixir for eternal life. Instead of making a life elixir, they blew themselves up in a massive laboratory explosion. They had accidentally learned the secrets of saltpeter, a critical component of the substance called gunpowder. A revolution in weaponry was about to begin. China was about to bring a gun to a knife fight.

FIRE LANCES

Sooner or later, somebody was bound to build something that combined the thrusting power of a spear with the hilarity of an ignited fart. That somebody was the Chinese, and the something was the fire lance—the world's very first gun. It was little more than a bamboo tube filled with gunpowder and strapped to a spear. It had only one shot, and its range was poor, but anyone standing in front of an exploding fire lance would definitely know they'd been hit. Not only could the tube spew flames for a brief moment, it could be loaded with iron shrapnel or poison gas, giving the target even more to worry about. It's unclear how effective this great-great-grandpa of the firearm was, though it was probably somewhere between a sparkler and a curling iron on the firepower scale, with most of the actual killing being done with the spearhead. On the other hand, the explosions of the fire lance certainly would have scared the enemy, who must have thought the Chinese had summoned the power of ancient fire demons to their bidding.

DATE OF ORIGIN: Possibly as early as 900 CE
IN WIDE USE BY: Twelfth century
OTHER NAMES: *Huo qiang*
(pear-flower spear)
PRECURSOR TO: Fire tube (a more powerful version with a metal tube); cannon; handgun
ADVANTAGES: Some physical damage; *huge* psychological effect
DISADVANTAGES: Relatively weak firepower due to the bamboo tube; only fires one shot
USER REVIEWS: "Why did someone ruin this perfectly good spear by strapping it to a sparkler?"

ROCKET ARROWS

The first gunpowder weapons were little more than arrows with a small packet of gunpowder strapped to them. A fuse was lit, the arrow was shot from a bow, and its target was set on fire by the exploding incendiary device. This invention, first used in 228 CE, marked a very mild beginning to a long, exciting history of bombs and firearms. Several centuries later, one of the emperor's scientists thought outside the box: "Hey! I just realized something—what if we use the explosion to propel the arrow? It'll make the arrow go a lot faster, and we can throw the bow away." And that's precisely how that shit went down. In 969, the Chinese generals Yue Yifang and Feng Jisheng used gunpowder to propel their arrows, culminating in the world's first rocket launchers. These rockets became more powerful and elaborate, and by the fifteenth century, the Chinese and Koreans were using massive gunpowder-fueled contraptions that could fire hundreds of arrows at once. No straw hut was safe.

DATE OF ORIGIN: 969 CE
INVENTED BY: Generals Yue Yifang and Feng Jisheng (who probably stole all the credit from their researchers)
PRECURSOR TO: Korean *hwacha*, a mobile rocket arrow cart

THE FIRST BOMBS

Gunpowder in and of itself is not necessarily a weapon. If ignited, it instantly goes up in flames with no percussive blast. But as Jin-era Chinese chemists were discovering, if said gunpowder is packed into a tightly sealed iron container, it makes a "heavens-shaking thunder crash" that can scatter you limb from limb. You could try to throw these early grenades with your hand, but they were heavy, and there was always the risk that they would roll back to you and blow off *your* ass à la Wile E. Coyote. But it just so happened that in the mid-thirteenth century, the counterweight trebuchet (or "Muslim trebuchet," as the Chinese knew it) had made its way to China. All of a sudden, the army of the Jurchen Jin dynasty could blow up enemy houses that were really far away. They could also pack the bomb with poison shrapnel to amplify the carnage. This was perfect for dealing with aggressive dicks like the Mongols, who were starting to step off the steppe and step up to the Chinese.

DATE OF ORIGIN: 1231
DEVELOPED BY: Song and Jin dynasties
MADE FAMOUS BY: Wile E. Coyote
USED WITH: Trebuchet

LANDMINES

When you hear *landmine*, you probably think of that Metallica video with the crazy mute guy in the hospital bed. But did you know landmines were actually invented by the Chinese, way back in the thirteenth century? True story. The Song dynasty was deathly afraid of the emerging Mongol threat. (They were right to be afraid, too, since the Mongols would swoop in and conquer them in just a few years' time.) A bright Chinese officer named Lou Qianxia came up with a solution: a big underground bomb that would blow the hooves right off the invading Mongol horses. The Chinese developed two types of trigger: (1) an "ambush" type, which relied on Chinese soldiers lying in wait and igniting the bomb just as the enemy was approaching the minefield, and (2) a more sophisticated mechanism that was triggered by enemy movement. In the latter version, an enemy's foot would press on a plate, which released a pin, which caused a weight to fall into an underground trench. The falling weight would pull on a cord, which would spin a wheel, which would act as a flint, creating sparks that would ignite the bomb fuse. It was a lot like the game Mouse Trap, only it could blow your balls off.

DATE OF ORIGIN: 1277
ADVANTAGES: Makes enemy more tentative; can be deadly if enemy happens to stand on the giant X
DISADVANTAGE: Early fuses took a while to ignite
PRECURSOR TO: Wheellock musket, which used the same flint-wheel firing system

GENGHIS KHAN WILL STEAL YOUR SHIT AND KILL YOU WITH IT

The Mongols were not an inventive people, per se. They didn't create jaw-dropping technologies like the Chinese. They didn't discover the path to enlightenment like the Hindus. They didn't blaze the spice trail like Marco Polo. They didn't accumulate a wealth of knowledge like the Arabs. And they kind of lifted their entire modus operandi from Attila the Hun. While everyone else was off creating, the Mongols were wandering aimlessly in Bumblefuckistan, eating meat and drinking horse blood. They didn't even really have homes! One day, their leader Genghis Khan became so completely jealous of everyone else and their accomplishments that he decided to take a big massive dump on the entire earth. His Mongol horsemen began to stomp through neighboring countries, ruining everyone's Sunday dim sum. Some people were able to use their technologies to keep the Mongols at bay, but not for long. Even if you could beat him, Genghis Khan was so stubbornly vindictive that he would eventually return and kick your ass. How did he manage to do it without knowledge and science? Easy. He captured the nerds who knew the science, and made them work for him. He'd use the landmines and bombs and trebuchets of other cultures against them, proving that while the Khan didn't have much book smarts, he certainly had a strong appreciation of irony. With a pace that remains unmatched to this day, the Mongols seized almost all of Asia (except for Japan, where a tsunami beat them down) and most of Eastern Europe. Genghis Khan enjoyed the spoils, too. He did so much fornicating that an estimated 8 percent of everyone liv-

ing in the former Mongol Empire is descended from his seed (roughly .5 percent of the entire world!). But the Mongol Empire didn't last long. Just like Sid Vicious, they were destined to die by their ferocious live fast/die young approach. Their hegemony began to crumble, leaving them with nothing but thousands of horses. With the magic of their empire gone, the Mongols returned to being crazy homeless people with too many pets.

ZHANMADAO

Suffice it to say there was no PETA in Song-era China. That's why they could develop the *zhanmadao*—a seriously cruel invention whose name literally means "horse-chopping saber." Even though eleventh-century China was loaded with explosives, it still felt the need for traditional weapons to use once the smoke had cleared. The zhanmadao wasn't complicated; it was basically just a big-ass sword that had evolved from previous large blades. You didn't need to be particularly skillful to use it—just grip it with both hands and hack. But you did have to have balls, as the zhanmadao required its wielder to crouch and wait for horses to rumble toward him in an ominous cloud of thundering death. At the last moment, if the warrior hadn't been trampled to death by the approaching cavalry, he would swing the zhanmadao and take one or two legs from the enemy's horses. After the horse collapsed, the zhanmadao wielder would then turn his horse chopper on the rider, who would be lying battered and dazed somewhere nearby. It was a brutal end for both horse and rider, but is it really anything you didn't read in *My Friend Flicka*?

DATE OF ORIGIN: No later than 1072
FAMOUS VICTIMS: Mongol horses, Jin dynasty cavalry
EVOLVED FROM: Dao
USER REVIEWS: "Did you see me?! I totally just cut that horse in two!"

Chapter 9.

JAPANESE BEEF:

SAMURAI VS. NINJA

800 CE–1700

I F YOU THOUGHT the Yankees and Red Sox had the greatest rivalry in history, you really need to read up on the martial history of Japan. The samurai and the ninja—two of the world's most recognizable warriors—were both born from the chaos of Japan's feudal era. And they could both kill the fuck out of the entire Yankee and Red Sox active roster. These vastly different warriors from two diametrically opposed social classes would clash physically and politically over the centuries. They would create a long-standing beef that would make baseball look like . . . well, baseball.

IN THIS CORNER: SAMURAI

Sometime around the eighth century CE, Japan's wealthy elite decided they were not wealthy and elite enough to solve the country's problems. The ruling landowners needed tax revenue, and they needed someone to collect it. Two prominent clans—the Taira and the Minamoto—began to draft soldiers to serve as law enforcement. These were essentially the first samurai. Their ranks would grow as more and more rich fucks hired samurai to fight someone else's samurai. Even though they stomped nuts all over Japan, samurai were ostensibly bound by a strict code of ethics called *bushido*. The primary tenet was loyalty to one's master. A samurai would rather die than see his master disgraced. In fact, dying was expected. This meant the warrior needed to overcome his fear of death by

constantly meditating on the prospect of meeting his demise. On the other hand, the samurai also knew that he was an untouchable one-man wrecking crew, and that the odds of someone else cutting him down in battle were slim to none.

KATANA

It may not look like much to the desensitized youth of today. Let's face it—the *katana* is one of the weakest weapons in the *Grand Theft Auto* games. But believe this: The katana was a *killing machine* in its time—the Cadillac of bladed weapons. Perhaps the finest sword ever created without divine intervention. What made the katana so special? Speed. As battles were increasingly fought in tight quarters, combat became faster. Blades became lighter and sleeker. A katana had to be drawn and cut a man in half in one fell swoop. Any time a new blade was forged, it had to pass this test. In fact, the biggest jerks in the samurai community would wander around town, looking for some hapless peasant to be their test subject. If the sword was able to behead the peasant and still retain its edge, it was considered a fine weapon. If it broke or became dull, it went back to the blacksmith. Forging was a complicated and highly ritualized process that involved several artisans. Most importantly, it involved heating and folding reinforced steel many times over. The more times the steel was folded, the stronger—and purer—it would become. Steel with high carbon content was harder and kept its edge but was more likely to break. Steel with small amounts of carbon was more malleable—less likely to break but more likely to bend. The Japanese learned to use the harder steel for the edge of the sword, and the softer steel for the core, resulting in the perfect flesh-cleaving utensil. The katana was the hottest knife of all, and anyone not clad in heavy armor was warm butter.

EASE OF USE: ★★✦ (complicated footwork to learn)
PEAK ERA: Sengoku period (mid-fifteenth to early seventeenth centuries), when the Japanese fought each other like rabid snow monkeys
USED WITH: *Wakizashi* (see page 131) or *tanto*
EVOLVED FROM: Japanese *tachi*, which was slightly larger and curvier
BEST DEFENSE: Remain indoors anytime a samurai gets a new katana

NAGINATA

Half spear. Half saber. All badass. The *naginata* was one of the oldest arms of the samurai. Early prototypes date back to the eighth century CE, when it was possibly invented by warrior-monks called *sohei*. The monks didn't have the luxury of horses, so they needed something to counter the cavalry that was constantly stomping holes in their temples. As the monks discovered, if you needed a really long sword to chop some horsemen down, the naginata wasn't a bad choice. You could plant the butt of the weapon in the ground, point the blade at the horse as it's galloping in, and blammo—massive horse wreck. The naginata gave its warrior a sizable reach advantage without weighing him or her down like the *Ōdachi*, a ridiculously oversized broad sword. This also made the naginata a favorite among Japanese women, who finally had an answer to all those marauding man-bullies who had pushed them around for so many centuries. The naginata was so widely used by women it eventually became known as the woman's spear— able to cut down thieves and rapists without the lady ever having to come near them. It was handed down from mother to daughter as an heirloom, so that even little girls could kick your ass with a naginata.

SIZE: Typically between five and eight feet long

USED BY: Women, samurai, and sohei, primarily from the tenth through sixteenth centuries

EVOLVED FROM: Possibly from the Chinese *kwan dao*, possibly from a farming utensil, possibly invented by sohei monks

EFFECTIVE AGAINST: Horses, rapists, and horse-rapists

WAKIZASHI

Let's be honest: some weapons get all the glory, and some weapons do all the dirty work. The *wakizashi* is the latter: a sidearm, always living in the shadow of its big brother the katana, and never getting the limelight. Together, the katana and wakizashi form the *daishō* of the samurai—one big sword and one little sword. But the katana was always the prima donna of the two. It was far too precious for the samurai to use on anything other than battle, out of fear of damaging it. Any sort of menial work—such as cutting off the head of a dead opponent, committing seppuku, or chopping up dead whales—was considered beneath the katana. That's where the wakizashi came in. To be fair, L'il Wak did see its fair share of indoor fighting. For one, it was considered offensive for a samurai to wear his katana indoors, but wearing the smaller wakizashi was completely kosher. So there were times (while the katana was waiting outside, signing autographs) that a fight would break out and a samurai would have to use the wak to gut somebody. It was even *better* to use the wakizashi in some circumstances, the tight space of Japanese living quarters being one. But for the most part, the wakizashi was always the Oates to the katana's Hall.

DATE OF ORIGIN: Between 1332 and 1369
USED WITH: Katana
SIMILAR TO: *Tanto*, an even smaller knife that sometimes accompanied the katana
USED FOR: Indoor fighting; seppuku; decapitating opponents; murdering sea urchins

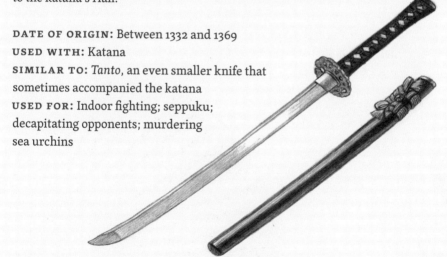

TESSEN

Don't be fooled. The *tessen* may look like an ordinary Japanese folding fan, but it's been used as a secret surprise weapon for centuries. Seriously. The cloth of the tessen usually conceals hard iron strips that, when folded, make a small handheld club that can knock you out cold. Others have the tips of the iron ribs sharpened, with the open fan acting as a graceful artery-slicing razor in the right hands. Why the need for this gentility and cuteness? Simple: when a samurai is barred from taking his katana inside a building, he keeps the tessen in his belt, knowing that he's always got a backup plan if shit gets hairy. I mean, who's going to tell him he can't have a fan? Remarkable as it may sound, this deadly samurai surprise has saved more than a few lives. One Takeda Shingen used a war fan to deflect the sword of a rival commander who had broken into his tent to assassinate him. So next time your host asks you to remove all your weapons before entering his house, remember to keep your tessen in your belt.

BIRTHPLACE: China
ALSO USED TO: Signal troops, deflect arrows
MADE FAMOUS BY: Samurai; that chick from *Mortal Kombat*; the Kyoshi warriors from *Avatar: The Last Airbender*
ADVANTAGES: Secret James Bond–style sneak attack! Can save your life in a pinch.
DISADVANTAGES: Won't penetrate armor; obvious limitations against hardcore weapons; makes you look like a big lady

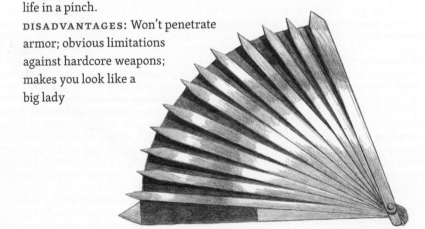

KAKUTE

Believe it or not, sometimes a samurai doesn't want to kill someone. Sometimes a quick, sharp, stabbing sensation in the pressure points is all that is needed to silence an unruly peasant. This is what the *kakute* was made for. Worn on the middle or index finger, sometimes with a second one on the thumb, the kakute was applied to the wrist, hands, or throat of a criminal—not to injure, but to subdue. It's much like the firm pinch a stern mother would give a misbehaving child. Though the pain of the kakute's spikes in a criminal's wrist was normally enough to make him shape up, the samurai could take the weapon a step further if he wanted to. Turn the kakute around, and you've got a nasty spiked knuckle-duster ring to pummel somebody with. Now even the wimpiest limp-wristed slaps turn into bruising body blows. Try this on your big brother next time he gives you a "titty twister."

EASE OF USE: ★┃ (some knowledge of pressure points required)

OTHER NAMES: *Kakushu* ("horned jewel"); *kakushi* ("horned finger")

ADVANTAGES: Concealable, nonlethal

DISADVANTAGES: Nonlethal

FUN FACT: Ninja use these too, so don't get cocky

IN THIS CORNER: THE SHINOBI (OR NINJA)

While the samurai were the nobility of feudal Japan, the ninja had their roots in the peasant class. If samurai were the paragon of honor and bravery in the face of death, then ninja were the dirty, lowdown, get-out-alive-at-all-costs types. While the samurai thrived on honor and glory, ninja thrived on people not knowing they existed. And in that, the ninja succeeded, because the truth is we don't have a lot of historical documentation of ninja activities. In fact, the very existence of ninja is somewhat difficult to prove, which is *exactly* the way the ninja would want it. You could say the surest proof that ninja exist is the fact that there's no proof of them existing!

The mystery surrounding the ninja may be due to the strict secrecy of their trade. It could also be the Japanese didn't consider them worth writing about. Ninja practiced espionage, infiltration, and secret assassination—subversive activities that were seen as shameful by the Japanese. But the ninja had to operate this way. If they faced a samurai in an open, honorable fight, they'd be hacked up and eaten with sticky rice. The only way a ninja was going to take out a samurai was if he decapitated him in his sleep. This required some highly specialized weapons.

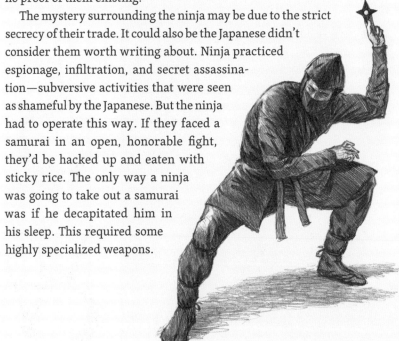

SHURIKEN

Historically, these weapons were used by ninja in surprise attacks. Today they're most commonly used by unsupervised children who inadvertently send a friend to the emergency room. *Shuriken* could be any number of small, bladed weapons used for stabbing or throwing. They were originally carved from everyday items, such as coins, carpentry tools, and washers. But the most famous shuriken is the *hira*, or "throwing star," as it's known to uncultured Westerners. Though the novelty of a thrown weapon might give the attacker an edge of surprise, the shuriken should *never* be one's primary weapon in a fight to the death. If your opponent is wielding a katana and you come at him with nothing but a shuriken, your ass will be torn up like a parking ticket. The shuriken was never intended to act as a "kill" weapon. It's more of a screening weapon, like the jab of a pugilist. The ninja would use the distraction of the shuriken as an opportunity to flee, or possibly as a chance to move in with a more serious weapon, like one of those new Chinese bombs.

LITERALLY MEANS: "Sword hidden in the hand"
VARIATIONS: *Bo-shuriken*—a spike-shaped dart
ADVANTAGES: Good for distraction and escaping
DISADVANTAGES: Isn't going to kill anybody

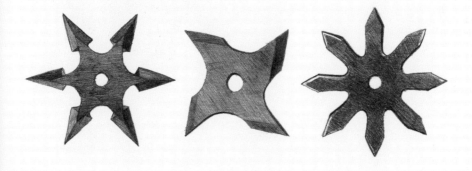

SHOKU

A ninja without *shoku* is like a hawk without wings. That's an ancient Japanese proverb that I just made up. When you witness the versatility and effectiveness of the shoku, you'll know exactly what I mean. The ninja used these spiked hand wraps to scale trees and other wooden structures. The shoku's curved claws would sink easily into wood to maintain the grip of even the fattest ninja. If while on his mission the ninja found himself face to face with an unexpected adversary, he already had a concealed weapon in his palms. He could use the shoku to slash, stab, or bludgeon his opponent, and he could even use it to catch his enemy's sword in midstrike. Some of the denser samurai mistakenly believed these ninja were catching sword blades with their bare hands. Ninja who wanted a matching set of spikes could save up their yen for some *ashiko* foot spikes. Then they'd have twice as much climbing power and twice as many ways to punch holes in their enemies. And if you aren't completely sold on the shoku yet, it can also be used in practical jokes. Just shake a friend's hand, and the shoku acts as a joy buzzer— only instead of buzzing, it severs metacarpal ligaments. Hilarious!

USED WITH: Ashiko (foot spikes)
ADVANTAGES: Can be used to climb trees and wooden structures; can be hidden in palm to use as a concealed weapon; can catch sword blades
DISADVANTAGES: Attempting to catch sword blades with the shoku can cause ninja to lose a hand if he has not been trained in this technique

KUSARI-GAMA

At some point, some ancient martial arts whiz figured out how to make the farming sickle even deadlier. Just attach a weighted chain to the handle and voilà—you have the *kusari-gama*. This would become one of the quintessential ninja weapons, a nice foil to a samurai's katana. Just use the weighted chain to entangle the opponent's sword or spear, then hack that clown to pieces with the sickle. You could also swing the sickle by the chain if you needed extra reach. You could even surprise the enemy by parrying with the sickle and belting him in the face with the weight. Just make sure you have plenty of open space to swing the chain. One notorious kusari-gama failure involved Yamada Shinryukan, a renowned kusari-gamist who was known for using the weapon to kill swordsmen. While engaged in a duel with an adversary, Yamada was led into a bamboo thicket only to find out he had no room to swing the chain of his kusari-gama. Unable to trap his foe's sword, Yamada was thoroughly screwed. His weapon was worthless in this setting. He was killed in the bamboo thicket, serving as an important reminder that home field advantage is everything.

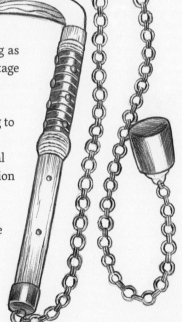

EASE OF USE: ★★★★ (exotic and confusing to everyone not trained in ninjutsu)

ADVANTAGES: Surprising, versatile; can deal blunt damage, slashing damage, or strangulation

DISADVANTAGES: Needs ample space to be effective

SIMILAR TO: The *kama*, an Okinawan sickle weapon; the *manrikigusari*, a chain weapon with a weight on each end

BEST DEFENSE: Always have lots of bamboo around

METSUBISHI

Not to be confused with the Japanese car of almost the same name, the *metsubishi* was one of the most deceptively effective weapons of the ninja. The word literally means "to crush the eye," and for all intents and purposes, it did exactly that. Metsubishi was a blinding powder, traditionally made of irritants like crushed pepper, salt, sand, ashes, broken glass, or iron filings. It was typically blown into the enemy's eyes via a hollow tube, thrown with the hands, or flung from the scabbard of a sword. Once the substance was dispensed into the eyes of the target, the ninja had a couple of valuable seconds to strike (or make a getaway) before the victim regained his or her sight. In a pinch, the ninja could forego the formality of prepared substances and grab anything nearby, such as a handful of dirt or an angry cat. Actually, throwing a cat at someone's eyes is probably more effective than traditional metsubishi. Use that instead!

EASE OF USE: ★
OTHER NAMES: "Ninja mace"
USED WITH: Hollow tube, hollow wooden box, sword scabbard
ADVANTAGES: Will stall one's enemy for a couple of seconds
DISADVANTAGES: Enemy will probably be very angry, so it's best to disappear before sight is recovered

FUKIYA

This blowgun is one of the simplest pieces of ninja weaponry. Just coat a few darts in your favorite poison or tranquilizer, load them into the reed, and hide in some bushes. Then comes the hard part of any sniper mission: sitting still and waiting for your enemy to get close. And with the poor range of the *fukiya*, you may have to wait a while. But the good thing about this particular weapon is it doubles as a snorkel. You can plant yourself in a nearby pond or moat and wait all damn night if need be. (But seriously, don't wait all night. You'll be covered in mosquito bites.) Once your enemy is within comfortable blowgun range, it's time to ready your weapon. Take a deep breath, steady your aim, and let loose with a big exhale. If your poison is strong enough, this might be enough to take out the target right away. But most likely you'll be using this as a distraction—like the shuriken—so while your enemy is dealing with the dart in his neck, it's best to rush in and finish the job with your sword. You did remember to pack a sword, right?

ADVANTAGES: Fukiya is a legitimate archery sport in Japan, so if your career as a ninja falls through, you can always fall back on that

DISADVANTAGES: You probably won't kill anyone with the fukiya, unless you dip your darts in anthrax. And even then, it will probably take a couple of days.

ALSO USED AS: Snorkel, flute

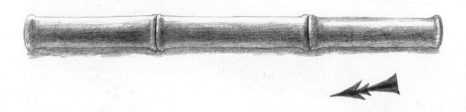

NEKO-TE

Female ninja, or *kunoichi*, were trained somewhat differently from their male counterparts. They used their gender to their advantage, often dressing as geishas, prostitutes, and performers. They relied heavily on impersonation skills and seductive prowess—like a deadly combination of Rich Little and Sharon Stone. These feminine wiles afforded the kunoichi easy access to places that the male ninja couldn't go (such as, ahem . . . bedrooms). As a result, these lady ninja tended to specialize in poisons and shurikens, keeping their distance and avoiding detection whenever possible. If a kunoichi's cover was blown and things did get physical, the female ninja relied heavily on *neko-te*, or "cat hands." Worn on the fingertips, the neko-te could be used as a last resort to attack the soft spots of an enemy—like the crotch and eyes—before getting the fuck out of Dodge.

USED BY: Kunoichi (female ninja)
USED WITH: Feminine wiles
MADE FAMOUS BY: That evil mutant chick from *X-Men 2*
USER REVIEWS: "I thought I was being a pretty convincing prostitute, but he found out I was a ninja, so I gouged him with my neko-te and got the hell out of there."

OKINAWAN WEAPONS

The people of the Okinawan archipelago weren't samurai or ninja. They were a separate ethnic group who spoke their own language, practiced their own religion, and made their living trading with the seafaring peoples of East Asia. But once the Japanese began to take an interest in Okinawa, things changed. Okinawans were forbidden to own weapons, leaving them defenseless against the samurai who had come to their islands to enforce the shogunate's laws. The people of Okinawa came up with a unique solution to the problem: they took simple everyday utensils and made them into samurai-stomping tools of pain. They developed their own martial art—*kobudo*—to serve as a template for using these weapons. All of a sudden, it became a lot less fun to fuck with Okinawa.

SAI

As you might expect, a sharpened *sai* can leave a pretty deep hole in somebody. But Okinawan police used them in a variety of nonlethal ways too, with the weapon acting as more of a truncheon than a dagger. This made the sai ideal for beating a person within an inch of his life but not completely killing him. A sai is held in one of two grips: with the prong facing out, or with the prong tucked into the forearm and the butt of the weapon facing out. Either end can be thrust into the solar plexus of an enemy, knocking the sweet breath of life from his wind sacs. (If the blow doesn't kill the target, he'll probably wish he were dead, as he struggles to suck air back into his collapsed respiratory system.) A kobudo master can flip between the two grips rapidly, much like a baton twirler in a marching band. The forks on the sides are great at catching attacks from swords and staffs. Once a strike from an opponent's weapon is blocked, the sai is twisted so that the attacking weapon is trapped between the middle and side prong. An experienced wielder can use this hold to break his enemy's weapon, or make him hit himself in the face with it like a mean older brother. "Why are you hitting yourself, you little puss?" he might say.

BIRTHPLACE: Most likely the Indonesian island of Java, where it is called the *chabang*

MADE FAMOUS BY: Raphael of the Teenage Mutant Ninja Turtles; Elektra of the *Daredevil* comics

ADVANTAGES: Excellent for defensive purposes; can parry attacks or disarm an opponent

DISADVANTAGES: Most modern sai are too blunt to kill anything

FUN FACT: Many kobudo warriors carried a third sai to throw at their opponents

NUNCHAKU

The nunchaku—or nunchucks, as they're known in America—are one of the most intriguing of the East Asian weapons. Never before has a weapon been so flashy—so dazzling to look at—yet so ineffective in actual combat. They don't have the reach of a bo staff. They lack the instant finishing power of a katana. And they have tremendous potential to harm the wielder. That's a 10/10 for style, 2/10 for effectiveness. But before we get into an argument about whether nunchucks could or couldn't fuck you up, let's take a look at their mysterious origins. It was once widely believed that nunchaku began as rice flails and were converted to weapon use after the weapons ban. Another legend has them originating as horse bridles that were modified for combat. Still another says they were developed as a means of folding and concealing a bo staff under one's clothing. The most likely origin is that nunchucks were brought to Okinawa by Chinese immigrants. In fact, the name nunchaku is derived from the Japanese pronunciation of the Chinese word for "two-sectioned staff." But that origin story is a real snoozer. So let's go with this one: Nunchucks were created by a resourceful Okinawan janitor who had to fight his way out of a pagoda using nothing but a broom and an iron chain. He broke the broom handle in half, attached the pieces with the chain, and commenced to beating ass. *Hwaaaah!*

EASE OF USE: ★★★★
VARIATIONS: Sticks can be smooth or have octagonal edges for more damage
MADE FAMOUS BY: Bruce Lee
ADVANTAGES: Looks cool; will totally get you laid
DISADVANTAGES: Will also totally get you killed
USED WITH: *"HWAAAH!"* sound

Chapter 10.

EW! WHAT'S THAT BOIL ON EUROPE'S NECK?!

1300–1500

FOURTEENTH-CENTURY Europe was not a place you'd want to live. Despite what you've seen at Medieval Times, the late Middle Ages was not a time of high adventure and wine goblets. Rather, it was a time of bubonic plague, torture, and dissenters' heads mounted on pikes. The Black Plague quickly spread across the continent, bringing an excruciatingly painful death via large neck boils and grotesquely swollen genitals. This pandemic was due to the aforementioned dumbasses who threw their feces in the street. The shit brought rats, who brought fleas, who brought the Black Death—wiping out a third of the European population. And as if that weren't enough, Europeans seemed hell-bent on reducing their population even more. France and England became embroiled in a hundred years of war, and some nutjobs in Spain began to shove hot pokers into the rectums of nonbelievers. Weaponry was getting more sophisticated, too. Even in a suit of full plate armor, nobody was safe.

MORNING STAR

Apparently the flanged mace wasn't brutal enough for some people. Sometime in the early fourteenth century, a sadistic German arms maker thought it would be a good idea to replace the flanges with sharp metal spikes. These new spiked maces could crush bones just like their ancestors, plus now they could puncture the flesh and tear off large chunks of skin. The enemy was left feeling like he'd been hit in the head with a hammer and mauled by a tiger at the same time. Though the morning star was ideally used on an enemy's head, the spikes allowed it to penetrate the links of a chain mail hauberk (a long shirt of armor). This meant that any body part the morning star connected with was going to be permanently disfigured. The Germans named this horrifying new weapon *Morgenstern* ("morning star"), proving that at one point in time, they definitely had a sense of humor. The Germans weren't the only ones to give a lovely euphemistic name to such a barbaric weapon. The English gave it the lofty moniker "holy water sprinkler." The Flemish variation of the spiked club was called the *godendag*, literally meaning "good day." Warfare had finally found what it had been missing: a sense of sarcastic courtesy.

DATE OF ORIGIN: Early 1300s
MADE FAMOUS BY: Fifteenth-century Germans
VARIATIONS: Godendag (Flemish), holy water sprinkler (English)
USER REVIEWS: "I love my new morning star. But I don't love cleaning bits of scalp from the spikes. There's got to be a better way!"

ESTOC

Blunt force wasn't the only way to deal with heavy armor. One could attempt to pierce it. But this presented difficulties, both in puncturing the metal and dislodging the puncturing weapon. Another strategy was to make weapons more slender with the hope of squeezing between the steel plates and links. One such weapon was the French *estoc*—a long, slender sword built exclusively for penetrating armor. Shockingly, the estoc had absolutely no cutting edge, which probably got a lot of laughs in the knight community. But its fine tip could slip through the smallest opening. The cross-section of the blade was shaped like a diamond or triangle that widened toward the base—the perfect design for wedging open chain mail links. So even though it was probably amusing for a knight to see a weird, pointy stick poking at him on the battlefield, it was probably less amusing when the estoc found an opening and punctured the knight's vital organs. Now who's laughing, stupid knight?

DATE OF ORIGIN: 1300s
PRECURSOR TO: Rapier
ALSO CALLED: Tuck (English); *Panzerstecher* (German)
SIMILAR TO: "Mercy dagger," a slender blade designed specifically to fit through the eye slots of a fallen knight's helmet; rondel, a conical dagger
ADVANTAGES: Can slip through openings in almost any armor; diamond shape acts as wedge to force open chain mail
DISADVANTAGES: No edge. Wielder must be very skilled and accurate to hit "soft spots"; must also be patient enough to wait for openings; must have thick skin to deal with jeers and insults from knights who don't consider the estoc a real man's weapon.

BUCKLER

In the early medieval era, it was common for a warrior to go into a fight with a heavy meat cleaver in his right hand and a big clunky shield in his left. By the late Middle Ages, however, swordplay was becoming more sophisticated. It was starting to be more about finesse and technique—no longer just a sport for testosterone-laden jocks with battle-axes. Swords were getting sent to fat camp, and they were coming back slender, lighter, and faster. The new swordsman needed something other than that big clunky shield he was lugging around. He also needed something that looked like a boob. The buckler was exactly what he looking for. Rather than being strapped to the arm like the shields of old, this new shield was held in the hand. It was lighter, more maneuverable, and sloped on the front to deflect blows. The buckler became every bit as much a fencing weapon as the sword that was carried in the right hand. It was less of a shield and more of a steel boxing glove. The wielder could use it to punch, keeping the buckler in his opponent's face like a jab. It could also be used to parry, disarm, or knock his opponent off balance. Some bucklers were produced with a sharp spike in the center, making them look even more like boobs. Swordplay suddenly got a whole lot steamier.

DATE OF USE: 1200–1600

USED WITH: Single-handed sword, rapier

EVOLVED FROM: Shield

ADVANTAGES: Light, fast, looks like a tit

DISADVANTAGES: Small, may not provide much coverage against arrows, wielder must be fast to use effectively, some people may call you a puss for using a tiny shield

PRECURSOR TO: Parrying daggers

VARIATIONS: Spiked buckler; square buckler, which had sharp corners for slicing

MAUL

If there was one thing peasants had access to, it was the tools of manual labor. Some of these, such as the maul, could easily be used in warfare with little or no conversion. The maul was a heavy sledgehammer used to drive carpentry stakes, so what it could do to the soft extremities of the human body goes without saying. There's no real technique when using a maul—just swing hard, preferably at the head or knees. Your opponent is guaranteed to feel the blow, even through a motorcycle helmet. In the fourteenth century, the maul was used as a weapon by rioting French peasants. A century later, the English military stole the idea from the French and stocked their own arsenals with mauls. In the Battle of Agincourt, the English archers used mauls as secondary weapons, scrambling the brains of their French opponents, who probably regretted turning the maul into a weapon in the first place.

EASE OF USE: ★★ (strength required)
USED BY: French peasants, English archers
TYPE OF DAMAGE: Smash!
MADE FAMOUS BY: *Donkey Kong*; that "ring the bell" strongman game at carnivals

WAR HAMMER

Unfortunately for knights, another weapon was emerging to deal with massive plate armor. This one was called the war hammer, and it had a bachelor's degree from the University of Knight-Stomping, with a major in Fucking Up Armored Dudes. The first war hammers were made with flat heads, dealing pure blunt force to everything they touched. But eventually a set of claws was added to the hammerhead, allowing the hammer to grip armor more easily. This ensured that every strike did maximum damage and prevented blows from glancing off the plates. In the right hands, this new, improved war hammer could rip apart the strongest armor in seconds flat. Even if the armor wasn't breached, it could be bent and misshapen to the point that the knight lost mobility in his joints. That's when the hammerer would flip the weapon over and use the pick, which could easily puncture armor when swung with full force. But there was risk involved in piercing the armor—the pick would often get stuck in the victim, leaving the warrior without a weapon for a couple of seconds. This was typically when the other knights would run to their buddy's aid and kill the hammerer with their longswords.

LENGTH: Typically under two feet
VARIATIONS: The *bec-de-corbin* ("crow's beak"), essentially a longer version of the war hammer
ADVANTAGES: Can break bones, even through plate armor
DISADVANTAGES: Can get stuck in plate armor, leaving the wielder defenseless
USER REVIEWS: "Does anyone have a spare war hammer? Mine got stuck in that knight's head."

Calling Bullshit
THE SPIKED FLAIL

In the fourteenth century, heavily armored knights began to run unchecked across the land, stealing the lunch money of everyone in Europe. The peasant class was left scratching its lice-infested head, trying to think of creative ways to kill this plate-armored juggernaut. One way was to use the threshing flail—a farming tool that had been modified for battle. It was simple: two pieces of iron-studded wood, hinged together by a couple of metal rings. The Hussites, a band of fifteenth-century Czechs, used the hell out of this segmented whacking stick. They cracked so many noggins with it that it became their national symbol. The iconic spiked "ball and chain" flail, on the other hand, seems to be largely a work of fiction. Though it's one of the coolest-*looking* weapons ever to come around, it was severely impractical. In order to use the spiked flail effectively, the wielder would have had to keep it in constant motion, spinning it around his body like a chain whip. There was always the distinct possibility of the flailer hitting himself, his friends, or his horse with his own weapon, resulting in an *epic flail fail*. Some flail supporters even claim that the weapon could generate more force than a hafted morning star, due to the extra length of chain. This claim is particularly bullshitty, since one could achieve the same force by simply lengthening the shaft of his morning star. In fact, the weapon with the solid shaft would probably generate more force, since the flail's chain absorbs some its momentum. So the next time you see a guy carrying one of these at the Ren Faire, do everyone a favor: push him over, hit him in the head with a morning star club, and tell him to put a solid shaft on his weapon.

EASE OF USE: ★★★★ (you're going to get very tired and very injured)

SIMILAR WEAPONS: The threshing flail, which is decidedly *not* bullshit

ADVANTAGES: Looks awesome; intimidating to face in battle

DISADVANTAGES: Difficult to control, *exhausting* to use

MADE FAMOUS BY: Liars at Renaissance Fairs; Millhouse, who accidentally knocked out that guy in the army surplus store on *The Simpsons*

SWORD BREAKER

Believe it or not, some people prefer not to go into a fight with a shield or buckler in their left hand. Who knows, maybe they just don't like being alive? If you're one of these people, I highly recommend investing in a parrying dagger. These nifty little left-handed blades came in a variety of shapes and sizes, many having elaborate crossguards and elegant quillons (those things that protect your hand). The sword breaker, on the other hand, comes with deep, ferocious teeth in the back of the blade, like an open crocodile mouth that's just daring you to step inside. This doesn't just make the dagger look awesome—it also serves a practical purpose.

The swordsman parries with this side of the dagger, hoping to catch the opponent's sword in the teeth. If successful, the wielder can twist the sword breaker to—you guessed it—*break the enemy's sword*. But unless the enemy was using a sword made of peanut brittle, this probably didn't happen too often. More likely, one would use the sword breaker to trap the enemy's weapon and pull it from his hand. Sure, it's less awesome than actually breaking the sword, but it still got the job done.

ADVANTAGES: Looks cool; can trap enemy's sword in its "teeth"

DISADVANTAGES: Probably won't actually break enemy's sword

RELATED TO: *Main gauche*, a left-handed parrying dagger used with the rapier; "trident dagger," a parrying dagger with two more blades that spring out from the sides

HALBERD

The Swiss have invented some pretty amazing things over the years: chocolate, cuckoo clocks, and money laundering, to name a few. But let's not forget the halberd, the steel-cleaving polearm of the Swiss Middle Ages. How effective is a halberd against a knight in full plate armor? Put it this way: if a knight were a lobster, then the halberd would be the cracking utensil that pulled the succulent meat from its shell. This bad boy of a polearm features at least three ways to ruin a knight's day. The axe can be swung in large sweeping angles, generating enough force to separate limbs from torsos. The hook on the back is used for grappling. As impregnable as steel plate is, it's bulky, and presents lots of corners for the knight's enemy to snag. Simply use the halberd hook to grab on to a piece of the knight's armor, and you can pull him around like a show pony. Once you've got the knight in a vulnerable position, use the pike on the top of the halberd to puncture his breastplate. Better yet, use this pike to catch him coming in on the horse, and you won't have to worry about fighting him at all. But don't miss. If the knight is fast enough to get inside the reach of your halberd, you're going to be considerably fucked.

DATE OF ORIGIN: Late 1300s

FAMOUS VICTIMS: Duke of Burgundy

ADVANTAGES: Versatile and powerful; can spear, grapple, and chop effectively

DISADVANTAGES: Like all polearms, it's not ideal for close combat; user can't carry a shield

MADE FAMOUS BY: The Swiss, who also make hot cocoa and neutrality

SIMILAR TO: Pike (a big metal infantry lance used to stop cavalry); *voulge* (a similar axe-like polearm); *fouchard* (same thing only different)

ENGLISH LONGBOW

While the rest of the world was making composite bows out of horn and sinew, the English were kicking it olde schoole. They made self bows from a single material, usually from yew, ash, or elm. After the wood was cured in a four-year process, it was used to make a resilient bow with a ton of stored energy. Simply put, this weapon could knock a knight off his horse at two hundred yards. But more than that, the longbow was a volume weapon—while the crossbow could fart out one or two rounds per minute, a trained English longbowman could shoot about twelve, and he could shoot them with accuracy. But training for the longbow was a bitch and a half. It required a lifetime commitment, with English boys typically beginning their archer lessons at around seven years of age. Over the next ten years, these lads would learn to pull a bowstring with a draw weight of over a hundred and fifty pounds. The training of these longbowmen was so famously hardcore that their skeletons have been found to have deformities in the arms and hands. (Insert masturbation joke here.) These highly skilled English archers first made a name for themselves during the Hundred Years' War, particularly the battles of Crécy and Agincourt. Even when outnumbered, they released volley after volley of bodkin-tipped arrows (a special diamond shape used to pierce armor), bringing the wrath of Her Majesty the Queen down on the forces of Frenchdom. The longbow remained relevant even during the early phases of firearms, until the French got their revenge by blowing the English to smithereens with their newfangled cannons.

EASE OF USE: ★★★☆ (lifetime of training required)
BIRTHPLACE: Wales
USED WITH: Bodkin-tipped arrows, which could penetrate chain mail and could allegedly pierce plate armor at close range
ADVANTAGES: Volume! And accuracy.
DISADVANTAGES: Hardcore training regimen fucks up your skeleton; made obsolete by firearms

MANCATCHER

Sometimes a knight didn't want to splatter somebody's blood all over the green grass of Normandy. Sometimes he wanted to capture the person alive, so he could collect a ransom or bounty. In this case, the knight might want to slip a mancatcher around the victim's neck. This wretched piece of weaponry is essentially a giant metal claw with spikes inside. It's allegedly nonlethal, though you can easily see how a guy could impale himself while trying to work free of the spikes. After a victim was subdued by the mancatcher, the knight would typically bind the person's hands for the ride home. Or if he was feeling like a dick, he might leave the person inside the jaws of the mancatcher for the entire horse ride. Ouch.

USED ON: Nobility; anyone with money; disorderly drunks

SIMILAR TO: *Sasumata*, the Japanese "spear-fork"

USER REVIEWS: "If I remove the mancatcher from your neck, do you promise to stop screaming?"

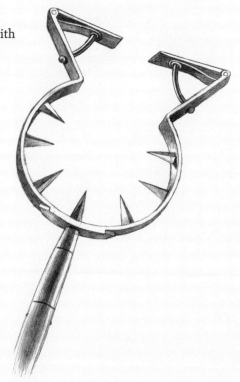

SHILLELAGH

Everyone knows the Irish love themselves some fightin'. Historically, if they weren't pummeling each other with fists, they were whacking each other upside the heads with knobby, wooden sticks. These sticks, known as shillelagh, have a mythical origin almost as old as Ireland itself. The story goes that when the Celts and Normans first invaded Ireland, they were considerably larger than the indigenous people who were already living there. Some of these "wee folk" didn't assimilate into the new Celt or Norman society. Instead, they would whack the invaders with sticks and disappear into the forest.[L] The conquerors began to refer to these tiny folk as *leprechauns*.[L] They would soon discover that the munchkins also had magical powers and golden treasures, and would fix your shoes if you left them on your doorstep.[DEFINITELY L] Whatever legendary origin you want to believe, the fact is that shillelagh fencing was a longstanding tradition in Ireland, lasting well into the nineteenth century. The rod was later modified to serve as a walking stick for travelers who needed protection on the road. It was used to settle disputes in a gentlemanly manner, especially at county fairs, where all kinds of friendly territorial violence would erupt. If you wanted to fight dirty, you could fill the head of your stick with lead for a "loaded shillelagh." Surprisingly, these stick fights resulted in very few serious injuries, with the winner typically helping the loser to his feet and buying him a round of whiskey.

DATE OF ORIGIN: First documented in the 1300s
BIRTHPLACE: County Wicklow, Ireland
PRONOUNCED: Shuh-LAY-leh
MADE FAMOUS BY: Leprechauns; the Notre Dame Fighting Irishman
USER REVIEWS: "Oh, fer fook's sek, ya wanker! I'll hit yeh with me whacking stick!"

L = Legend

CLAYMORE

As far as big-ass two-handed swords go, the claymore is probably the most famous. It got its big break in the 1990s, when it was cast as the star of Mel Gibson's *Braveheart*. Before long, the claymore had gone Hollywood. It had completely forgotten about its humble origins in the Wars of Scottish Independence. Back then, the claymore was much smaller and didn't yet have the amazingly cool crossguard that we associate with the sword. Over the next couple of centuries, the claymore put on some serious length, eventually becoming as long as a short adult male. Swords of this length were terrors on the Highland battlefields. In a melee fight, the claymore could keep the British troops from closing the distance, chopping them into haggis before they could get close enough to use their longswords. The Scottish Highlanders could even break armor and shields with this thing, and they swung their claymores with such ferocity that the handles needed spiral leather wrappings for the warriors to keep their grip. But wielding such a manly weapon does have its drawbacks: You don't get to carry a shield, which makes you vulnerable to attacks from the infamous English longbow. And in the event that you have to flee quickly from a volley of longbow arrows, you'll probably have to drop your heavy claymore in order to haul ass.

DATE OF ORIGIN: 1400s

BIRTHPLACE: Scotland

GAELIC NAME: *Claidheamh mòr* (don't ask me for the phonetic spelling)

MADE FAMOUS BY: Mel Gibson, who defended Scotland's independence for over two hundred years

ALSO AVAILABLE: Basket-hilt, or "clamshell" hilt claymore

SIMILAR TO: *Zweihänder*, the big-ass two-handed German sword of the sixteenth century

BOMBARD

Throughout the thirteenth and fourteenth centuries, firearms slowly made their way across the Middle East and Europe. These were mostly weak cannons like the *pot-de-fer* ("iron jug"), which queefed out a metal arrow every few minutes. Gunpowder was not a significant factor in European warfare until 1453, when the Turks showed up at Constantinople with the biggest guns the world had ever seen. The largest of these came to be known as the Great Turkish Bombard. It was a massive mofo that required ten thousand men and seventy oxen just to get it to the fight. Instead of arrows or bolts, these Turkish monster cannons fired large iron balls, some of which weighed over a ton. After bombarding the walls of Constantinople for two solid months, the Turkish army easily poured through the gaping holes in the city walls. They kicked the crap out of the Holy Roman Empire (which at that point was feeling more like the *Holey* Roman Empire, am I right?). Black powder weapons were no longer just noisy firecrackers that scared horses—they were thunderous tubes of death that could level civilizations.

EASE OF USE: ★★★ (requires a massive team of operators)

DATE OF ORIGIN: Smaller bombards in the 1300s, serious bombards in the 1400s

EVOLVED FROM: Pot-de-fer, the weak-ass queef cannon of the French and English

FAMOUS EXAMPLES: The Great Turkish Bombard; Mons Meg (Scottish); the Tsar Cannon (Russia)

MATCHLOCK ARQUEBUS

The earliest handheld firearms could barely put a dent in a well-crafted suit of plate armor. But by the middle of the fifteenth century, handheld firearms started to get a little more powerful. The badly named arquebus was one of the earliest matchlock firearms, meaning it was fired by touching a match to a hole. It was the first gun to be widely used by European militaries, since it could pierce the plate armor of a knight. Granted, at a distance of more than a few yards, the shot of the arquebus would probably bounce off a piece of decent plate. But at close range, an arquebusier could send Sir Lancelot to the mausoleum. Adding to the frustration of knights everywhere, the arquebus didn't require a lifetime of training like the English longbow. It must have killed the knight—both literally and figuratively—to be brought down in battle by a serf who was shoveling shit in a stable three months ago. This is why the arquebus would become the bane of chivalry. It wasn't nearly as accurate as the longbow. It was slow as hell to reload. And yeah, it could easily explode in the hands of the person trying to use it. But it wiped the smirks off the faces of medieval knights, and the shit-shoveling peasants got to laugh for once in their miserable lives.

EASE OF USE: ★★✦ (requires some training; user must have dry gunpowder)

DATE OF ORIGIN: 1400s

PRECURSOR TO: Wheellock firearm

ADVANTAGES: Doesn't require years to master; can be fired from narrow holes during siege defense; scares the bejesus out of enemy horses

DISADVANTAGES: Inaccurate; can't be used in rain; low-velocity shots won't pierce plate mail at long distances; slow to reload; might blow your hand off

Chapter 11.

MEANWHILE, IN THE REST OF THE WORLD . . .

AMERICAS, AFRICA & POLYNESIA
1300–1700

BEFORE THE SIXTEENTH CENTURY, Europeans gave little thought to what was going on outside their own precious continent. Google Maps hadn't been invented yet. And since people thought the world was flat, perhaps they figured there wasn't much point in wondering what was happening out there past the edges. Or maybe they were just self-centered assholes. Either way, there *were* things happening in the far corners of the world, and a lot of it was just as bloody and barbaric as anything the Europeans could come up with. These undiscovered heathens were creating highly effective weapons of their own. Sure, many of these guys didn't have metal, leaving them to rely on materials like wood, bone, pine cones, and other stuff you'd find in a compost bin. But don't snicker: these weapons *worked*, taking down no shortage of tribal adversaries, wild game, and, soon enough, wandering white men.

MACUAHUITL

The Aztecs ruled central Mexico from roughly the fourteenth to sixteenth centuries. They were crazy as hell, engaging in mass human sacrifice and fighting other Mesoamericans the way modern men fight going to the proctologist. Aztec warriors often wore brightly colored feathers and jaguar-skin jumpsuits. If that didn't scare the shit out of the opposing fighters, then the *macuahuitl* in the warrior's hand definitely would. As we discussed in Chapter 1, obsidian is the black glass of death that can separate heads from bodies, and the macuahuitl is covered in it. This weapon is sometimes referred to as the Aztec sword, though that's not entirely accurate. The obsidian edges do cut like a sword, but part of the macuahuitl's power comes from its girth. The mass of the club delivers the impactful blow of a mace, and the obsidian razors in the edge of the weapon provide added slashing damage. It's essentially two weapons combined into one strange, brutal razor-paddle. The macuahuitl is so brutal and so razory that an Aztec allegedly decapitated a conquistador horse with it. One can assume the conquistadors probably invoked the wrath of the white man's god and shot the horse-killer in the face with a gun. Then took his land, enslaved his people, and wiped them out with exotic viruses. So, even-stevens, then.

DATE OF ORIGIN: Early versions in Mayan reliefs, circa 600–900 CE

ADVANTAGES: Very sharp edges; can also be used as a club

DISADVANTAGES: Obsidian bits often break or dislodge on impact; much slower than a sword

HARPOON

On the other end of North America, way up at the top of the map, life was very different. The Inuit people of the frozen north preferred killing whales instead of each other, and the harpoon was the preferred method of whalicide. Harpoons were used way back in prehistoric times. They were fairly simple but so effective that they quickly spread to every arctic culture, including those of Scandinavia. Now I know what you're thinking: "Harpoons are for spearing whales and fish. You can't use those on people." Well, keep living in your little fantasy world, pal, because if it can mirk a large sea mammal, it can mirk you, too. Inuit harpoons were typically comprised of barbed "toggling heads," meaning once the victim was impaled, the tip of the harpoon would break off and turn askew. This made it impossible to remove. From there, the prey had nowhere to run. The hunter would pull on the attached cord, haul the victim in, and crush it to death with a club or walrus—whichever he had on hand.

USED BY: Ancient Thule and Inuit tribes; Scandinavians

FAMOUS VICTIMS: Whales, seals, and salmon

EVOLVED FROM: Spear

PRECURSOR TO: Harpoon gun, which is even more awesome

USER REVIEWS: "Dying like a fish is totally embarrassing!"

TOMAHAWK

When someone says "American Indians," the first three things most people think of are Pocahontas, broken treaties, and the tomahawk. No other weapon is so emblematic of Native Americans, and no other weapon was more valued by them. The ancestors of the tomahawk were ancient monolithic stone clubs—single pieces of flint that were chiseled into rough, hatchet-like instruments. Over time, the construction became more sophisticated, with the flint blades becoming finer and the handles becoming separate pieces of timber. After the arrival of the white devil, Native Americans began using iron-bladed tomahawks, which were most likely acquired in trades with French explorers. Tomahawks could generate savage power with relatively compact bodies, making them great for close-quarter combat. These hatchets weren't exclusively for fighting, either. A tomahawk could be used to chop wood or drive stakes into the ground, and some models featured a built-in pipe that allowed the warrior to blaze up between battles. This pipe-and-tomahawk combo became a visual reminder of the dual possibilities of war and peace. Instead of fighting, you could always smoke a bowl with your palefaced conquerors and get along with them—for approximately three hours. Then as soon as the pipe part of the tomahawk was empty, you'd be right back to splitting skulls with the other end.

DATE OF ORIGIN: 1500s

ETYMOLOGY: Algonquin

MADE FAMOUS BY: Every Western movie ever made

EVOLVED FROM: Monolithic stone clubs

ALSO USED AS: Domestic tool; rallying cry for assholes at Atlanta Braves games

THROWING KNIFE

Generally speaking, throwing your knife at an enemy is a bad idea. Best-case scenario: the knife lands, and you're left without it. Worst-case scenario: the knife misses, and your enemy picks it up and stabs you in the neck with it. But let's face it—throwing knives is too badass *not* to do. The Native Americans knew this, too. That's why they carried more than one with them—so they could chuck one off and still have one left. The earliest Native American knives were made of flint. Even in these precolonial days of stone tools, the indigenous Americans were honing their throwing skills. Spot an enemy, hold your knife between your thumb and three middle fingers, generally by the end that has *less* weight. Then—*fwoooop*—throw it at your target. Knife throwing can be done in an end-over-end rotating manner, which requires the wielder to carefully judge the distance before throwing, or in a shot-put style, which produces no rotation at all. Either way requires a shitload of practice but, if done correctly, should leave your enemy surprised (and dead).

EASE OF USE: ★★★ (this is going to require some practice)
EVOLVED FROM: Throwing sticks
ADVANTAGES: Bad as hell
DISADVANTAGES: You lose a knife

SCALPING OR HEADSHRINKING

Which Is Better?

If you're an aspiring Native American warrior, chances are you'll want to keep a trophy from the battlefield. In North America, this usually meant scalping—removing a piece of the victim's scalp with one's knife. But the Shuar people of South America practiced the art of headshrinking—an elaborate, mystical process that was done to avenge the death of a loved one. Both practices are intended to fortify the mojo of the slayer by giving him the life force of the slain. But alas, most people only have one head. This means you can't both scalp *and* headshrink your victim. So which should you choose?

SCALPING:

Pro—Easier to do than headshrinking. All you need is a knife and a head.

Con—Some other warriors might think you're lazy for not cutting off the whole head.

Pro—Lots of cultures have practiced scalping, which makes it a *tad* less barbaric in the eyes of the world. In fact, many scholars say that most Native American tribes didn't begin scalping until European settlers did it to them first.

Con—Victim can actually *survive*. Nothing's creepier than seeing your old scalping victim walking around town with his skull exposed!

Pro—Owning a severed scalp is kind of like having a pet.

Con—Your dog is probably going to end up humping the scalp.

HEADSHRINKING:

Pro—You get to consume *natema*, a concoction made from hallucinogenic herbs. This allows you to visit the spirit world so you can see which person is responsible for killing your loved one. You also get to *trip balls*.

Con—Shrinking the person's head is a long, disgusting process that involves lots of intricate steps: removing the skin from the skull, treating the skin in hot water, drying it, molding and sewing, etc. And all of this must be done while coming down off the natema. Bummer.

Pro—Warrior can sell shrunken heads to sadistic white collectors, like the Ripley's Believe It or Not! Museum.

Con—Most countries have clamped down on shrunken head trafficking, so the head might be difficult to sell. It will probably just end up cluttering your apartment.

Pro—Great for Halloween. Spooky as hell.

Con—If you forget to sew the mouth shut, the head's spirit can call for vengeance against you. Plus, the spirit will hang around all day without chipping in for rent.

GUNSTOCK CLUB

The Native Americans already had an impressive arsenal of clubs before the Europeans arrived. The ballheaded club was a juggernaut of a head-cracker that was said to be strong enough to knock men's brains out. Then with the arrival of the colonial musket came the inspiration for the gunstock club. One can only assume the Native Americans observed the Europeans using the butts of their guns as bludgeoning weapons and thought, "Holy crap. How come we can't make one of those?" The natives went right to work, tossing aside their outmoded ballheaded clubs and fashioning wooden clubs in the form of these musket butts. Some of the more clever artisans affixed a flint, bone, or iron blade to the club, allowing for stabbing attacks as well as clubbing. And unlike the stock of a real musket, it wouldn't fall apart after two whacks. If attacked by an angry Lakota with a gunstock club, your best defense was to run until you found a real gun.

EASE OF USE: ★↗

DATE OF ORIGIN: 1600s

EVOLVED FROM: Ballheaded clubs, which were already plenty effective

INSPIRED BY: European musket design

MADE OBSOLETE BY: Gunstocks with guns attached

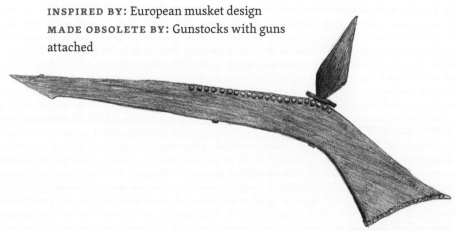

LEI O MANO CLUB

At the risk of generalizing, let it be known that Hawaiians love a good scrap. Centuries ago they developed their own martial art known as *lua* and came up with some bitchin' weapons to go along with it. One of the most infamous was the shark-tooth weapon, or *lei o mano*. The most well-known of these was the lei o mano war club. If you could swing a shark by its tail and beat someone with it, you'd have captured the essence of this weapon. Made from a large oval-shaped chunk of koa hardwood, the lei o mano club would be brutally effective without the addition of shark's teeth. But those nasty bits of barbed calcium are what made this simple war club into a primitive chain saw—and it didn't even require gasoline. All a Koa warrior had to do was land the toothed edge anywhere on the opponent's body and let the chompers of nature's premier aquatic predator do their work. Not only are shark teeth sharp, but they're also slightly hooked to keep prey from escaping their grip. When dragged across human flesh, they definitely leave marks. And when driven by the inertia of the heavy Koa club, they devastate. It's not uncommon for the teeth to become dislodged in a victim. Getting beaten by a shark-tooth club was probably second only to being eaten by an actual shark.

VARIATIONS: *Hoe lei o mano* (shark-tooth oar); *ku'eku'e lei o mano* (shark-tooth knuckle-duster)

ADVANTAGES: Like a Stone Age chain saw; club is effective as a blunt instrument even without the teeth

DISADVANTAGES: Teeth can fall out on contact (still leaving the warrior with an effective albeit toothless hardwood club); angry sharks might pursue user to ends of the Earth

MAKA PAHOA KO'OKO'O

This big wooden fork is not made for eating. It's the "pronged spear" of the Hawaiian Koas. In fact, the prongs on this spear are spaced just far enough apart to do lots of mean things. They can immobilize the opponent's weapon. They can be used to pin his arms and legs to the ground. They can be jammed around the neck for some serious windpipe damage. But most insidiously, the *maka pahoa ko'oko'o* can be used to *gouge out the eyes* of one's enemy. And if you're in a hurry and just want to go home and get to bed on time, you can finish your opponent with the sharp spike on its other end. Aloha, mf'er.

USED BY: Hawaiian Koa practitioners

ALSO AVAILABLE: *Maka pahoa lua*, the compact "pronged dagger" that fits in your purse

USER REVIEWS: "Can somebody pull these eyeballs off my maka pahoa ko'oko'o?"

TOKI

The *adze* is an obscure wood-chipping tool known only to Old English carpenters and Scrabble players. Apparently, the Maoris of ancient New Zealand thought up the adze too, and as far as I know, they're the only people in history who made it into a weapon. The *toki*—or "Maori fighting adze"—was a rarity on the battlefields of Oceania. It was typically a status symbol, worn only by tribal leaders. But if need be, it could be used in wartime executions. Its chiseled greenstone blade was the perfect instrument for lobotomizing enemy islanders, particularly if said enemy was already knocked down by a more substantial weapon. (Think of the toki as the Maori equivalent of the medieval knight's "mercy dagger" [see page 148], except with a perpendicular blade.) If you were captured by the Maoris in battle, execution by toki was considered an honorable way to go. Hey, it beats slavery.

ALSO CALLED: Maori fighting adze
USED BY: Maori leaders
USED ON: Wounded warriors; respected prisoners of war
FUN FACT: Just as a carpenter's adze was used for hollowing out timber, a Maori adze was used for hollowing out skulls

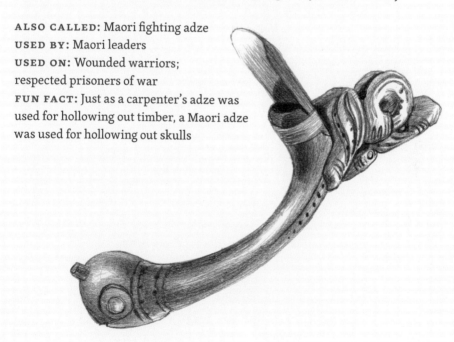

STINGRAY BARBS

Early on in the history of Pacific migration, some unlucky islander was the very first person to accidentally step on a stingray. One can imagine the stream of obscenities that came from that person's mouth as he began to realize his foot was impaled by a twelve-inch barb. After the person's friends helped him or her remove the barb, they must have started thinking, "Hey, I wonder if we could make that into a knife." And that's exactly what they did. The Oceanic islanders began using the painful barbed spine of the stingray to their own advantage, using it as a dagger blade or bundling several together to make a spear tip. Suddenly, these warriors of the South Pacific could turn opposing armies into an entire field of Steve Irwins. Once thrust into an enemy warrior, the stingray barb began to serve its natural purpose. It would easily break off in the wound, requiring careful removal. Suffice to say, if the target wasn't killed immediately, he at least had something on his mind for the rest of the fight. Such as "I hope to God our village surgeon is still alive."

DATE OF ORIGIN: A really, really long time ago
USED BY: Pacific Islanders, Australian aborigines, possibly Mesoamericans
ADVANTAGES: Breaks into tiny splinters once imbedded in target
DISADVANTAGES: Can only be used once
FAMOUS VICTIMS: Odysseus, whose son killed him with a stingray spear; "Crocodile Hunter" Steve Irwin
FUN FACT: If you find yourself stabbed by a stingray barb, science recommends you apply hot water to the wound. If the barb breaks off in the wound, science says you should go to a hospital for surgery. *Never* attempt to remove the barb yourself.

NGOMBE EXECUTION SWORD

Unlike most Native Americans and Polynesians, the ancient Africans did have metal. And they used it to make crazy-ass swords like the Ngombe execution sword. It's difficult to determine any practical application of this blade just from looking at it. Some historians say these swords were simply status symbols with no utilitarian function (bo-ring!). But others claim the Ngombe blade had a much more sinister purpose. European explorers often gave detailed—perhaps exaggerated—accounts of Congolese savages beheading prisoners with this sword. One harrowing piece of art shows a wide-eyed prisoner, arms bound to a chair, having his chin lifted by a rope collar as an executioner winds up to deliver his decapitating blow. Whether this scene was fictional or not, it contributed to the substantial mythos of the Ngombe sword, planting it firmly in the nightmares of visiting colonialists.

USED BY: Ngombe people of the Congo

ADVANTAGES: People assume wielder is either crazy or a tribal leader (either can be used to your advantage); can possibly behead people

DISADVANTAGES: *Heavy*; good luck lugging that around all day in the jungle

KPINGA

At the risk of sounding like a five-year-old, the *kpinga* might be the most awesomely rad weapon ever created. It's so cool that you can't stare directly at it without suffering an involuntary bowel movement. As a matter of fact, if you even *think* about the kpinga, it will feel your thoughts and fly at your face like a primitive heat-seeking buzz saw. Over the centuries, Africa has seen its share of awesomely rad throwing knives. Many of them feature multiple blades. This guarantees that when you throw the knife, it can land on any side and still stab the shit out of somebody. It also means that when the knife hits an enemy's shield, it has a tendency to rotate around the shield and kill its target anyway. And if it doesn't kill its target, the knife will probably kill one of the target's buddies. (And if it doesn't do that, it will surely cause great distress among the enemy.) This is why early European explorers described these blades

as thunderbolts that glistened in the sun and hummed through the air at their terrified prey. Some are even crafted to look like bird heads, so that while the victim is being murdered, he thinks he's being devoured by cockatoos. Alfred Hitchcock wishes he'd thought of this.

DATE OF ORIGIN: Uncertain, probably no later than the 1600s
USED BY: Azande people of Lake Chad
REGIONAL VARIATIONS: *Shongo* (from Zaire), *onzil* (the bird-shaped knife of Gabon), *hunga munga* (the "F-shaped" knife of Sudan)
MADE FAMOUS BY: Buffy the Vampire Slayer
ADVANTAGES: Rotates around shields; scares the shit out of enemies; makes any loser an instant badass
DISADVANTAGES: One assumes the enemy could pick up your thrown kpinga and take its badassedness from you

POISONED ARROWS

The Chinese and Europeans may have had saltpeter, but the people of sub-Saharan Africa had amazing biodiversity, including some of the deadliest toxins on earth. Europeans who arrived in the fifteenth and sixteenth centuries were aghast to see members of their parties fall prey to African arrows that were coated with these mysterious substances. The colonialists didn't know it, but they'd just had their first taste of strophanthin. Strophanthus plants—along with acokanthera, milkweed, and oleander—were widely used to make arrow poisons across the African continent. Their seeds were extracted and made into formulas by medicine men, and the resulting poisons could induce cardiac arrest in the victim unless he could quickly acquire all of the ingredients of the top-secret antidote (which was typically only known by other medicine men, so good fucking luck). It was common for archers to leave their arrow heads lodged in decomposing animal flesh to accumulate bacteria. The Kamba people of Kenya mixed strophanthus with scorpion venom. The Hausa people of western and central Africa threw in disgusting animal-based substances like monkey entrails, snake heads, pus from sores, and even menstrual fluid. So if the cardiac poison didn't kill you, the gross-out factor would.

EASE OF USE: ★★⸱ (requires archery skill *and* a medicine man)
FAMOUS VICTIMS: Nuno Tristan, who in 1446 became the first European to die from African poison arrows
FUN FACT: It's believed that some Africans immunized themselves to these poisons with gradual inoculations. Historians say they probably got the idea from *The Princess Bride.*

Chapter 12.

THE AGE OF DISCOVERY:

"I JUST DISCOVERED HOW TO BLOW YOUR HEAD OFF!"

EUROPE, 1500–1800

FOR CENTURIES, Europeans sat around with their thumbs up their asses while the East did all the thinking. For about twelve hundred years, between the fall of Rome and the Turkish siege of Constantinople, Europe wore the dunce cap. But in 1492, a brilliant discovery was made by one Christopher Columbus. He found out that you didn't have to be the first to get to something in order to claim it. Like the Dane Cook of the fifteenth century, Columbus laid claim to the continent that was sort of already found by Eric the Red, and was actually discovered many thousands of years ago by people who crossed the Bering Strait. But the past didn't matter. The Age of Discovery was here, and that meant that all previous claims were off! Europeans set sail to plant their flags all over the world and showed their lily-white asses to exotic nations near and far. And the brightest minds in the West were discovering new weapons to take along.

MUSKET

The arquebus (see page 164) forced medieval knights to become increasingly paranoid. Between battles, they'd hurry back to their blacksmiths and huff, "I need stronger armor! This will never hold up against the enemy's new firearms!" The smiths responded by making armor better and heavier until the knight could barely move. Arms makers, on the other hand, were trying to stay one step ahead. Completely out of ideas, they simply made the arquebus bigger and heavier. This new supersized arquebus was called the musket. In theory, it was a handgun, but in actuality, it was so powerful and unwieldy that it now required a forked stand to rest the barrel on. The musket wasn't much for accuracy, either. It shot heavy metal balls that didn't fit the barrel too snugly. When fired, the musket shot would bounce around the inside of the barrel before exiting the gun in an unpredictable direction. But this was the most powerful shot of its time for a standard infantryman. The musket could—if it hit its mark—blow through any type of armor. (Yes, nerds—that includes dragon scale.)

EVOLVED FROM:
Arquebus
AVAILABLE IN: Matchlock, wheellock, and later in flintlock
POWER: Greater than an arquebus, less than a cannon
MADE FAMOUS BY: Pilgrims, who used muskets to shoot turkeys; the British, who conquered the world with the Brown Bess musket; and the Three Musketeers, who, despite their name, never actually seem to be wielding muskets
BEST DEFENSE: Plug end of gun with finger

RAPIER

During the late Middle Ages, the European sword went in for some liposuction. It came back from the plastic surgeon looking sleeker, longer, and a whole lot faster. Plus, it felt a little bit better about itself. The ultimate result was the rapier—one of the feyest swords ever forged on the anvil. Though it is now relegated to foppish caricatures of seventeenth-century Frenchmen, the rapier was once the weapon of choice for skilled European swordsmen. The long, sleek blade and ornate hilt made it the fashionable choice of arms among dandy elites, giving the weapon the nickname of "dress sword." It wasn't just pretty—the rapier's decorative hilts protected the wielder's hand from opponents' blades, with the weighted ball on the bottom serving as a functional counterweight to the blade. The rapier was decidedly not a slashing weapon like the traditional broadsword, but rather a thrusting weapon. And it demanded fast footwork, which meant that most armor was out of the question. These limitations were a turnoff to some swordsmen, who preferred to ride into battle covered in steel and swinging a meat cleaver. In theory, those who mastered the elegant rapier could easily compensate with its reach and speed—provided they had years of in-depth professional instruction. The weapon's elitism would be its demise, however, as it eventually gave way to the lighter, and considerably lamer, "small sword." The successor may have been more practical, but it lacked the panache of the rapier. When was the last time you heard about someone having a "small sword wit"? Never, that's when.

EASE OF USE: ★★★☆ (lots of fancy learning involved)
DATE OF ORIGIN: 1500
EVOLVED FROM: *Estoc* (see page 148), longsword (see page 112)
ADVANTAGE: Classy, shows everyone you resolve disputes in a gentlemanly manner
DISADVANTAGE: Only for dueling; *not* for actual warfare. Seriously, you will get crushed.

BRONZE CULVERIN

As gunpowder became cheaper and stronger, the gunsmiths of the Renaissance became bolder. They attempted to shove more and more powder into their cannons to give them more bang. Unfortunately, many of these cannons were made of cast iron, which could easily explode and send shrapnel into any unfortunate sack of meat that happened to be standing nearby. Some gunsmiths found the solution in the weapons of the past—they started making their cannons from bronze, which was slightly more elastic. This meant that on a misfire, bronze cannons would tear or rupture, rather than explode like their cast-iron competitors. Bronze allowed gunners to experiment with larger doses of powder without fearing for their lives. They could achieve more power without resorting to the ridiculously large cannonballs of the bombard. Bronze cannons were also lighter than iron guns, and therefore more mobile. And if that weren't enough, the Renaissance saw another advancement in firearm technology: cannons began to increase in barrel length. The culverin featured a length-to-bore ratio of about forty to one, which generally meant it could shoot a helluva lot farther than other guns. Renaissance soldiers could knock down the walls of a city standing much farther away, sparing them the awkward moment of staring at the enemy while waiting for the cannons to fire.

DATE OF ORIGIN: 1500s
ADVANTAGES: Less likely to explode and kill user; bronze is light and portable; can shoot really far
DISADVANTAGES: More expensive than cast iron; longer barrel can be cumbersome on battlefield

FLINTLOCK PISTOL

Picture yourself as a single dude in seventeenth-century Paris. You really want to pay a midnight booty call to your favorite mademoiselle, but this means walking the streets after dark, all alone. *Les avenues* are crawling with muggers and bandits, and there's no real police force to protect you from them. But you're in luck, because your local gunsmith just made a big batch of flintlock pistols. Previous handguns were of the wheellock variety—much better than those crappy matchlocks, which required two hands. But even the wheellock had problems. It was complicated—winding the wheel required the use of an extra piece of equipment called a spanner, which would often end up lost in your chaise lounge cushions. Wheellocks also tended to break easily, meaning they were costly to maintain. Then came the snaphance mechanism (basically a simpler means of sparking the powder), which quickly evolved into the flintlock, which became every European civilian's best friend. It was affordable and dependable and could be concealed under the coat or at the waist. Robbers who preyed on people walking the streets at night suddenly had something to watch out for, as even the wussiest nobleman could be packing a flintlock pistol in his codpiece.

DATE OF ORIGIN: Early 1600s

EVOLVED FROM: Wheellock and snaphance pistols

PRECURSOR TO: Percussion cap firearms

USED BY: Civilians and military personnel, who could fire the one-handed pistol from horseback

FUN FACT: Flintlocks had their drawbacks, most notably their tendency to fire accidentally during the loading process. This is the origin of the phrase "going off half-cocked," which disappointingly did *not* come from a man with half a penis.

BLUNDERBUSS

You're on a ship that's being attacked. Your cannons have failed you, and the enemy is boarding your vessel. It's too late for cannonfire, and you're not close enough to whip out your cutlass. But you've got a perfect midrange surprise for your adversaries hidden under your frock—your blunderbuss. This flintlock pistol was a precursor to the shotgun, packing plenty of wallop for the unsuspecting invaders. Although a blunderbuss can't hit the broad side of a blue whale from eighty yards away, it does the job in the close quarters of a ship. The flared muzzle allows for easy loading in a pinch. Just shove in some black powder and metal pellets (or nails, rocks, broken glass, or whatever makeshift ammunition you can find) and fire. Odds are, at least one of your enemies is dead, and the rest are almost certainly terrified of the crude boomstick you've just produced. Take note: the blunderbuss has a powerful kick and is always fired from the hip, not the shoulder, unless the shooter wants to lose some teeth. Unfortunately, few weapons are as infamously maligned. Sure, blunderbusseses (blunderbi?) were used by explorers, stagecoach drivers, and pilgrims, but the weapon's primary image has been firmly cemented by Hollywood movies as the firearm of pirates. Many marauding buccaneers used the blunderbuss to wreak terror on hapless shore dwellers. Many a port was pillaged and many a maiden was ravished at the barrel of a blunderbuss. Arrrggh!

DATE OF ORIGIN: Early 1600s; used widely by 1700s

ADVANTAGES: Sprays out metal pellets, killing everything within a 45-degree angle

DISADVANTAGES: Might kill your own men (but how useful are they anyway?)

MADE FAMOUS BY: Pirates!

BRANDISTOCK

Stealth weapons have always made things more interesting, even if they weren't the most effective killers. The samurai had the tessen, the Chinese had the sleeve arrow, and Europeans had the brandistock. Allegedly carried by off-duty police officers, the brandistock appeared to be a walking cane or staff. But with a sharp motion of the wrist, this ordinary walking cane could deploy three retractable blades. Once the blades were shaken out of the shaft, they locked into place to become a vicious spiked polearm. The person you thought was "Giuseppe, the crippled guy from the bar"—was actually "Giuseppe, the guy with the hidden trident"! All of a sudden, you begin to regret some of the things you confessed to Giuseppe during long nights of drinking.

DATE OF ORIGIN: 1500s
BIRTHPLACE: Italy
ALSO CALLED: Feather staff
PRECURSOR TO: Seriously badass spy weapons
USED BY: Off-duty police officers, who might need to surprise-attack unruly drunks; unruly drunks, who might need to surprise-attack police officers

LANTERN SHIELD

The Renaissance may have resulted in some important cultural achievements, but it also resulted in some of the dumbest ideas to ever leak out of the human skull. One of the most absurd weapons to be forged during this period was the lantern shield—a horribly convoluted clusterfuck of a weapon. Yup, take a moment and absorb its retardedness. Who were the great military minds that came up with this one, and what the hell were they possibly thinking? The answer to the first question is *the Italians*, and the answer to the second question is *your guess is as good as mine*. First, let's start with the big sword protruding from the shield. This could have a practical use, as you could use your shield to stab as well as defend. Not a bad idea in and of itself, but then the lantern throws a couple more blades onto the steel gauntlet. "O-kay, lantern shield. Slow down," you say. But then it adds a steel gauntlet for your hand and a serrated blade to the center of the shield. (This was ostensibly to use as a sword breaker, though the odds of catching someone's sword with the blind spot in the middle of your shield are slim). But there's more! The best part of the whole lantern shield is the hook that allows you to hang a lantern on it, so you can temporarily blind your enemy should they attack you at night. There was a fine line between genius and insanity during the Renaissance, and the lantern shield landed on the wrong side of it.

DATE OF ORIGIN: 1500s
BIRTHPLACE: Italy
ADVANTAGES:
Excellent
conversation piece
for nutjobs
DISADVANTAGES:
Tries to do too many
things, does none of
them well

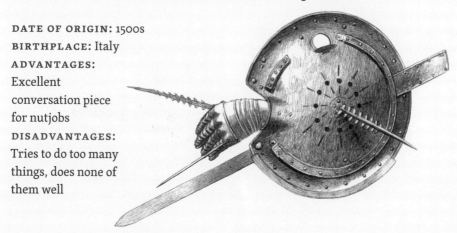

WOULD YOU LIKE A GUN WITH THAT AXE?

The Renaissance and early modern periods resulted in some pretty ridiculous weapon combinations. The thinking of the era was, "Hey, if two things are good separately, then they must be twice as good together, right?" In some cases, this was true. Early firearms took an eternity to reload, so it made sense to have another weapon that you could use in between rounds. Infantry would fire a volley of musket shot, then charge in and stab the enemy to death with their bayonets. This made sense. But the genie of the combination weapon was out of its bottle, and there was no putting it back in. The trend of hilarious hybrids continued for the next three centuries. Axes were combined with rifles, scimitars were combined with war hammers (really), and intercontinental ballistic missiles were combined with bullwhips (not really). The Apache was a favorite among Parisian gangsters of the nineteenth century. It looked like a set of brass knuckles welded onto the barrel of a revolver, with a switchblade underneath. Indo-Persian countries made shields with built-in guns. And someone even made spoons with flintlock pistols in the handles—presumably to teach shitty waiters a lesson.

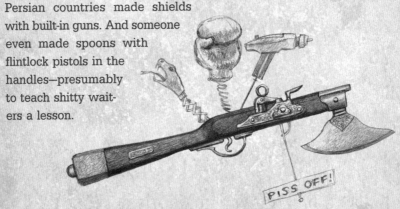

CHAIN SHOT & BAR SHOT

The late Renaissance ushered in an era of creative artillery as well. People were no longer slaves to the same old boring round cannonballs that they had used for two hundred years. Chain shot and bar shot took the artillery scene by storm, providing bored cannoneers with a new, exciting way to tear things apart. These innovative cannon shots were primarily used by naval vessels to wreck the masts and rigging of enemy ships. The bar shot would either have a solid bar or a telescoping one between the balls. The chain shot would expand to full length in flight. Both would take out a larger chunk of boat than a plain round shot. Occasionally, chain shot was also used to mow down wide swaths of infantry, who probably only caught a micro-glimpse of the long metal chain flying at them before they were divided in half.

DATE OF ORIGIN: 1600s

ADVANTAGES: Can take out ship masts, immobilizing the vessel so user can commandeer it

DISADVANTAGES: Less accurate than round shot due to its tumbling end over end; must be used at close ranges

MADE OBSOLETE BY: Armored steamships, which didn't have masts to destroy

PUCKLE GUN

In the seventeenth century, Muslim Turks were still mired in a seemingly eternal war with the Christian nations of Eastern Europe. One bright English attorney named James Puckle decided to do something to stop these swarthy "others" from invading fellow Caucasian lands. He invented the Puckle gun: the world's first machine gun. Puckle's "defence gun" looked something like a revolver that had been fed a steady diet of synthetic testosterone. It could fire about nine shots per minute, whereas the fastest musketeers of the time could only pull off about three. But that's not even the most remarkable aspect of the Puckle gun—it was also the world's first *racist* weapon. James Puckle, Esq., hated the Turks so much that he designed two versions of the weapon: one that fired round bullets to be used on Christians, and another that shot square bullets to use on Muslims (no shit!). The reasoning was that square bullets would ostensibly hurt the victim more. Only then, while dying in pain from the right angles of the square bullet, would the nonbelieving Muslim realize how much God hated him. Puckle's idea never quite caught on, but his defence gun had already set the bar high for machine guns and white Christian supremacy.

DATE OF ORIGIN: 1718
ALSO CALLED: Defence gun
USED WITH: Racist bullets, which inflict more pain on nonwhite targets
PRECURSOR TO: Dr. Klaussen's infernal Jew ray

THE GUILLOTINE
A Not-So-Instant Death?

At the end of the 1700s, the French Revolution was separating heads from bourgeois bodies at breakneck speed. One of the cooler heads of the time—Dr. Joseph-Ignace Guillotin—said, "Hey guys, we should at least make sure people aren't being tortured. 'Kay?" With that, he invented the infamous guillotine. Its slanted blade ensured a clean cut, removing the head in one swipe. This meant the condemned person would always die instantly, without pain . . . *right*? Not so fast. As beheadings became increasingly regular, spectators began to notice eerie phenomena. Tales began to circulate about the death of the famous chemist Antoine Lavoisier. Before being executed, Lavoisier had agreed to blink after his decapitation, for as long as he was lucid. Witnesses claimed he blinked for fifteen seconds after his head was separated from his body. Many view the Lavoisier story with skepticism. But, that still leaves us with the countless other stories of lucid decapitation. Charlotte Corday allegedly looked quite indignant when her severed head was smacked by the executioner. Other severed heads have been described as "attempting to speak." Some have moved their eyes and focused on people, as if responding to their names. Granted, there are also a number of stories of people who *didn't* respond after getting chopped. Isn't it possible that what we perceive to be cognitive responses are just the final gasps of the nervous system? Or are these "living heads" actually aware for a few seconds that they've been chopped? Scientists say there's no way of knowing, but they allow that it's possible for the brain to survive for about thirteen seconds without fresh blood. Gaaahh!

Chapter 13.

FAKIRS, THUGS & HEADHUNTERS

ASIA, 1500–1900 CE

BY THE SEVENTEENTH CENTURY, almost every place on Earth had been discovered. Europeans had pushed their way into Asia, and the exotic spices they found there were just what they needed to liven up their sucky Anglo-Saxon cuisine. A wealth of foreign goods began to pour into European markets, but the situation quickly deteriorated into a furious pissing match over which European country would get control over which Asian country. The English, Portuguese, Spanish, Dutch, and French all fought each other initially, then turned their weapons on the native ingrates who didn't want to be part of their empire. They would soon discover that these fakirs, thugs, and headhunters on the other side of the Earth had their own nasty heathen weapons—bizarre creations that no proper Englishman could have dreamed of. And they used them in ways the good Lord never intended.

PATA

This strange piece of cutlery was surely looked upon with derision by Brits who set up camp in seventeenth-century India. After all, it wasn't every day an Englishman saw a sword with its very own steel gauntlet built into the handle. Sure, the built-in gauntlet gave some protection to the wielder, but it took away all articulation in the wrist. This ran completely contrary to everything the Europeans had learned in fencing class. And to make it even weirder, the pata was held by a grip that ran perpendicular to its blade. Nonetheless, the pata became a favorite among the Sikhs, Mughals, Marathas, and Rajputs who fought for control of the subcontinent during this time. In fact, it was the seemingly awkward grip of the pata that allowed Indian fighters to generate such power with the sword. The pata drew on the strength of the forearm and upper body instead of the wrist, which meant anything it connected with was probably going to be divided in two. Highly trained swordsmen could also wield the weapon with surprising agility. It was common to see swordsmen showing off their skills at Indian festivals—sometimes by cutting in half a leaf that was lying flat on the open palm of a friend. Not bad for filthy heathen swordsmanship. In real combat, the pata was typically wielded on horseback, where the brace of the gauntlet may have allowed one to stab without breaking his wrists. It was equally handy for infantry to use against cavalry, with the warrior sometimes wielding a pata in each hand and twirling them around like a whirling dervish of horse-chopping doom.

DATE OF ORIGIN: 1500s, though not widely used until the 1600s

EVOLVED FROM: *Katar* (see page 91)

USED BY: Sikh, Mughals, Maratha, and Rajput warriors, especially from horseback

FUN FACT: Patas were often made with ferocious animal faces on the hilts, which made it look like the wielder's fist was a lion vomiting up a sword blade

FAKIR'S CRUTCH

The fakirs were originally a group of ascetics who practiced a mystical form of Islam called Sufism. They eschewed all luxuries, surviving entirely on alms and their connection with God, sort of like that guy Craig who sleeps on your couch for a month and never looks for a job. They were also forbidden to carry arms. This was problematic for them, especially since they had to sleep on the street. So like the Shaolin monks before them, the fakirs started to compromise their religious morals and look for ways to circumvent their ban on weapons. They began to develop hidden weapons that could be disguised as ordinary objects. (Hey, if it can't be seen by ordinary humans, then it can't be seen by God, right?) They came up with the fakir's crutch— a walking cane that concealed a nasty secret weapon. Though the crutch wasn't an ideal weapon to use in a battle, it could save the life of a fakir in a pinch. It was heavy enough to use as a mace, but its real power was the sharp blade hidden inside the cane. The fakir simply had to unscrew the handle and pull, and he had himself a small rapier that could keep him from being murdered by street thugs. He just had to remember to put the blade back in the handle when he was done so God didn't know he'd been playing with weapons.

SIMILAR TO: *Gupti*, the Indian sword cane
ADVANTAGES: Can save your life in a pinch; disguised as ordinary walking cane, so wielder doesn't compromise religious beliefs; even fools God
DISADVANTAGES: Some blades have to be unscrewed from the crutch, which can take considerable time during an attack

BAGH NAKH

If you ever get access to a time machine, you may want to consider visiting seventeenth-century India, if only to try out the *bagh nakh*. This dope-ass metal claw was about as close as mankind has ever come to actually becoming Wolverine. It could be worn over the knuckles in true Wolverine style or hidden inside the palm as a stealth weapon. Unfortunately, the people of medieval India didn't know what they had. They treated the bagh nakh with scorn, calling it a seditious weapon of thieves and assassins. There was a reason for this reputation, though. In 1674, a group of Maratha rebels was at war with the Bijapur Sultanate. The rebel leader Shivaji had accepted a meeting with Afzal Khan, the Bijapuri general. Shivaji got word that Afzal intended to murder him, so he came to the meeting strapped and armored. When the two leaders embraced, Afzal attacked with a *katar* (the Indian "punch dagger"), but failed to penetrate Shivaji's chain mail. Shivaji responded by disemboweling Afzal with a bagh nakh, which he'd smuggled into the meeting in his palm. The bagh nakh forever changed the course of Indian politics, as the Maratha rebellion soon grew into the Maratha Empire. The moral of this story: if you're planning on surprise-attacking somebody, there's a good chance he's planning on surprise-attacking you, too.

DATE OF ORIGIN: 1600s, possibly 1500s

INSPIRED BY: Tiger claws

FAMOUS VICTIMS: Afzal Khan, who had his guts plucked out by a bagh nakh

ALSO AVAILABLE: *Bich'hwa bagh nakh*, a bagh nakh with a dagger on the handle

ADVANTAGES: Concealable; turns wielder into fucking Wolverine

DISADVANTAGES: Must be used close to target; not made of real adamantium like Wolverine's claws

MADU

As time passed, the term *fakir* began to lose its Muslim association and came to mean "any raggedy-ass homeless person in India." Like the Muslim fakirs, the Hindu ones weren't supposed to carry weapons. They too became adept at making nontraditional arms, indicating that the Hindu pantheon must be as easy to fool as the Muslim deity. In addition to lying on beds of nails, the Hindu fakirs got really good at making weapons out of animal horns. "Fakir's horns" were constructed of two steel-tipped antelope horns pointing in opposite directions. These horns could be fastened to a shield to make the *madu*—a handy defensive weapon. The wielder could use the shield of the madu to block, and the horns to parry. If he wished to toss his religion out the window entirely, he could stab with the sharp tips of the horns, easily gouging the windpipe or eyeballs of his attacker. Madu weren't merely used by ascetics and beggars, either. They became popular with the Maratha military, who would parry with them in the left hand, while a sword or other traditional weapon was wielded in the right. In the hands of a pro, the blocks, parries, and attacks of a madu could happen so fast the enemy would think he'd been stabbed by the trident of Shiva himself.

EASE OF USE: ★★★ (awkward grip requires a surprising amount of training)
USED BY: Fakirs, yogis, Hindu beggars, the Bhil people of Central India
ALSO CALLED: *Maru;* "horny stabby shield"
SIMILAR TO: The *adarga*, which is the Moorish version of the madu; fakir's horns, which is a madu without the shield; antelope, which is an animal with horns but no shield
ADVANTAGES: Surprisingly useful; can block, parry, and stab (if your religion permits it)
DISADVANTAGES: Rhino-skin shield may aggravate allergies

THUGGEE LIFE

If you're planning a vacation in seventeenth-century India, there are some dangers you should be aware of—malaria, dysentery, and food poisoning from street vendors, to name a few. But there's one other peril that can sneak up and put a hurt on you worse than any food-borne illness. I'm talking about the notorious Thuggee cult that has plagued the subcontinent since the 1300s. You may know them from their cartoonish portrayals in such films as *Indiana Jones and the Temple of Doom*. Even though real Thuggees didn't rip still-beating hearts from victims' chests with their bare hands, they did murder many thousands of people over the centuries, all to satiate the supposed bloodlust of the Hindu goddess Kali. (Note: there are tons of Hindus who worship Kali and do not practice ritual mass murder.) How did they do it? The typical Thuggee approach was to gain the trust of a group of travelers, possibly offering to travel with them for more security. Little by little, more undercover Thuggees would join the party along the way. Sometimes the killers would walk hundreds of miles with the travelers, waiting for them to let down their guards. Then, when their numbers were sufficient, the Thuggee hitmen would slip their yellow handkerchiefs—called *rumals*—around the necks of their unsuspecting victims. Like an evil Indian A-Team, each member of the gang had his own function: some would create distractions, some would restrain the victims, and some might play music to drown out the sound of the crime. Thuggee life was exclusive to men. Fathers passed on Thug secrets to their sons, who were expected to make their own "sacrifices to Kali" at age eighteen. The cult died out in the 1830s, as travelers slowly learned not to trust people with yellow scarves.

KUKRI

This crooked Nepalese knife was the stuff of nightmares for British imperial forces. In the early nineteenth century, the English were busy suppressing a Gurkha uprising in Nepal, which they coveted for its wealth of abominable snowmen. British troops began to tell harrowing tales of tiny, ferocious Nepalese warriors appearing from the brush and hacking them up with small, powerful swords. These Gurkhas would strike with their kukris, taking off the arms and heads of the English in the blink of an eye. The attackers would then disappear into the forest before the British could say, "What's all this then?" How was this lowly dagger able to generate such power in such a compact body? By brilliance in design. The kukri was weighted toward the tip, meaning it could chop like an English chef chopped up sheep kidneys. It was also small enough to wield with great speed. And its sharp edge lay inside the curve—a shape that might have been derived from the Greek *kopis*. This meant that the blade actually hit its target sooner than it would have if it were straight. The British were so impressed by the Gurkhas and their kukris that they made a deal with Nepal: you send your guys to fight for us, and we'll leave you the hell alone. The Gurkhas became loyal allies of the British, and the British became firm believers in the power of the kukri. From that point on, they wore it as a sidearm, as a reminder of how they once got their asses kicked by the mountain men of Nepal.

ALSO CALLED: *Khukuri*
PRONOUNCED: KOOK-ree (Western); KOO-ker-ree (original)
EVOLVED FROM: Possibly Greek *kopis* or Spanish *falcata*
FAMOUS VICTIMS: British imperial soldiers
TECHNIQUES: Can stab, hack downward, or be thrust upward like the tusk of a boar
FUN FACT: The two small notches above the handle are to prevent blood from flowing onto the user's hand

PUNJI STICKS

Although this booby trap became famous in the Vietnam War of the 1960s, it actually originated in ancient times. Simple, mean, and sometimes deadly, *punji* sticks are the reason invading armies tread slowly through the jungles of southern Asia. First, bamboo is sharpened and fire-treated to hold its edge. Then the tips are typically treated with (get ready for this) *human shit*. Then the spikes are placed in the ground and concealed with grass or shrubs or placed under a trap door. Gravity is the only force needed to make the punji sticks work. When the unsuspecting interloper steps on them, the pain is severe. The victim might think he's been bitten by a cobra. And he'll soon wish he was—he can find a buddy to suck out snake poison, but good luck finding one who will suck out human feces. Once you've been stabbed with punji sticks, it's all downhill. The bacteria from the feces penetrates the wound and quickly causes infections. And since antibiotics are in short supply in eighteenth-century Asia, the punji stick victim will die a slow, agonizing death. Let's take a moment to give thanks for modern medicine, shall we?

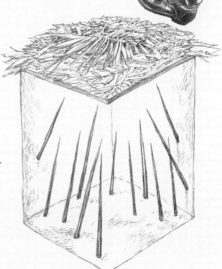

EASE OF USE: ★⸱ (gravity does most of the work; some whittling skills required)

MADE FAMOUS BY: Viet Cong

USED WITH: Feces

SIMILAR TO: *Troup de loup* (European spike trap, usually without feces)

BEST DEFENSE: Armored shoes

KRIS

No, this isn't the Kris who sells you weed at the local video store. This kris is the wavy blade of death that's synonymous with Indonesian warriors. Said to possess mystical powers, the kris is centuries deep in superstition. The original kris blades were made from a fallen meteorite. And since the ancients probably thought the meteorite was God's own testicle fallen from space, they assumed it was imbued with magical properties. Ever since then, each kris was thought to possess a spirit. The wielder had to feed this spirit by anointing his blade with oil or placing food next to it at night. Kris blades always had an odd number, signifying good luck for the user. While all that may be bullshit, the wavy edge served a utilitarian purpose—it ensured that the blade would sever the maximum number of veins and arteries on its way through the flesh, and it made it easier to plunge the knife between ribs. The askew handle of the kris also worked to the wielder's advantage, though it seems counterintuitive to Western swordsmen. It allowed the wielder to generate more thrusting power without bending his or her wrist, acting much like the *katar* of India. In fact, the Javanese believed the kris to be so powerful it could kill a person just by stabbing his shadow. Let's see *your* sword do that.

DATE OF ORIGIN: No later than the fourteenth century
BIRTHPLACE: Indonesian island of Java
PRONOUNCED: Keh-rees
ADVANTAGES: Wavy blade allows the knife to plunge easily between ribs; weapon can be handed down as family heirloom, so user's children can't bitch about how he never left them any inheritance
DISADVANTAGES: Spirit that inhabits the blade is a picky eater who always complains about the snacks you leave out

PARANG

The parang was a machete of sorts to the people of Southeast Asia. Their tropical habitats were so overgrown with woody plants that they needed the parang just to get out of their houses in the morning. But to the Dayaks of Borneo, this bad jungle knife had a more sinister purpose: removing heads from bodies. The island of Borneo has always been infamous for its headhunters, a group of aptly named warriors who admittedly enjoyed decapitating people from time to time. This practice may seem barbaric to Western eyes, but it actually served several useful purposes in Bornean beliefs. It brought a more bountiful rice crop. It allowed slaves to serve their departed masters in the afterlife. And if a young Dayak boy wanted to propose to a maiden, he couldn't pop the question without presenting her with a decent head. (Seriously.) If the young man was serious about marriage, he knew he had to dig his father's parang out of the toolshed and get busy searching the island for a nice-sized noggin.

BIRTHPLACE: Malaysia

SIMILAR TO: Machete

USED FOR: Weed whacking, head chopping

ADVANTAGES: Short blade designed to be drawn quickly for instant throat slashing; Dayak metal is supposedly quite good

DISADVANTAGES: Neighbors always borrow parang and forget to return it

FUN FACT: The pommel of the parang was often decorated with hair from previously hunted heads

KARAMBIT

The Javan tiger was a ferocious feline badass that stalked every living thing in Indonesia for thousands of years. The Javanese people were so impressed by the tiger's ability to rip through a wild boar carcass that they began to develop weapons to emulate the tiger's claws. Though the tiger itself went extinct in the twentieth century, we still have the *karambit* to remember it by. This strange, sickle-shaped dagger looks more like a meat hook than a sword. It's usually wielded with the index finger inside the ring for control, and the blade coming out of the bottom of the fist. This allows the wielder to punch upward or in a hooking motion toward the enemy's throat or torso. The karambit can also be used on a guy's testicles, which makes you wonder how any man could ever use such a weapon on another man. This is probably why the karambit is traditionally considered a woman's weapon—because women can emasculate a guy and not give a shit.

BIRTHPLACE: Indonesian island of Java
ALSO CALLED: *Korambit, kerambit*
USED BY: Javanese women; some men, as a last resort; Filipino warriors
ADVANTAGES: Hook shape allows for maximum damage in a compact blade; finger ring prevents weapon from being dislodged from wielder's hand
DISADVANTAGES: Enemy might accuse you of fighting like a girl, at which point you can rip off his balls and say, "Now who's the girl?"

BALISONG

If you've ever seen a movie about gangsters in the 1950s, you've undoubtedly seen someone flipping open a *balisong*. Better known as the butterfly knife, this strange clicking weapon unsheathes its blade with a twirl of the handle. The flipping techniques are often so elaborate that they resemble secret handshakes. So what exactly is happening during this odd combination of flips? The handle of the butterfly knife is hinged in two, concealing the blade in the middle. In order to expose the edge, the wielder has to swing one side of the handle around to the other side of his knuckles. The objective is to do this with one hand—not only so you can defend yourself with the free hand, but also because it looks cool. Where did this weird-ass flippy blade come from? The earliest documented design was found in a French magazine published in 1710, but unless you want to get your ass kicked by a Filipino knife enthusiast, you'll keep this to yourself. Filipinos claim the balisong is their invention, dating as far back as 800 CE. This makes the balisong high on our list of "Reasons Not to Fuck with the Philippines," second only to Manny Pacquiao.

EASE OF USE: ★★
(flipping it open is easier than it looks)
BIRTHPLACE: Possibly early eighteenth-century France; possibly ancient Philippines
MADE FAMOUS BY: 1950s street thugs, after the knife was imported by war veterans and Filipino immigrants
MATERIALS: Steel or buffalo horn, depending on the era
MADE OBSOLETE BY: The less complicated switchblade; state and federal laws, which have effectively made the balisong illegal

DEERHORN KNIVES

One single deerhorn knife is already loaded with ways to stab a person. But when wielded in pairs, the deerhorn *knives* become a ridiculously formidable means of personal protection that can leave one's adversary dead in the mud. Used primarily in the martial art of *baguazhang*, the deerhorn knives are a relatively recent invention. Dong Hai Chuan—the nineteenth-century martial artist who developed baguazhang—carried a pair of deerhorn knives for personal protection. He used the circular movements and evasive footwork of baguazhang to make the most of the multi-pointed blades. In his hands, these weren't stationary weapons but whirling razors that chopped up everything within arm's length. According to legend, Dong Hai Chuan could take on dozens of opponents at one time with his deerhorn knife/baguazhang combination. He could use the weapons together to trap larger weapons like spears and swords. Or he could use one blade to knock the attacker off balance, while using the other knife to counterattack. This is precisely how Dong Hai Chuan's countless adversaries met their ends. We can't say exactly how many enemies attacked Dong Hai Chuan, but we can assume it was a lot, since he worked as a tax collector for the emperor.

EASE OF USE: ★★★✦
(significant risk of injury to wielder; must be familiar with baguazhang techniques)
ALSO CALLED: Mandarin duck blades, crescent moon knives
EVOLVED FROM: Wind-and-fire wheels
USED BY: Baguazhang practitioners
MADE FAMOUS BY: Dong Hai Chuan, a fat Chinese guy who allegedly killed a buttload of people with deerhorn knives

SLEEVE ARROWS

These spring-loaded darts were a specialty weapon of Chinese assassins. The arrows packed less wallop than those of a typical bow, but they could do one thing most other weapons couldn't: they could get past security. Picture yourself as an assassin sent to gun down an important official in Qing-era China. Said official is probably going to be inside a heavily guarded fortification, and you're probably not getting your hand cannon past security. You need a stealth attack. You need something you can fit up your sleeve. Some sort of "sleeve arrow," maybe. Lucky for you, there is such a thing. It's little more than a powerful spring inside a metal tube. It's doesn't pack the punch of a musket. It's not going to penetrate armor or elephant hide, and it won't hack a person up like a dao. But it can kill an unsuspecting person from twenty feet away if he's not shielded. Just get close enough, wait for the right moment, then point your arm and pull the trigger. As for the escape plan . . . well, you're on your own there.

EVOLVED FROM: Back crossbow, a similar device that was worn on the back and fired while the wielder was bowing to his target

ADVANTAGES: Stealth, gets past security

DISADVANTAGES: Lack of power and range; you only get *one* shot; you'll probably be killed after shooting it

JEZAIL

Believe it or not, the grasping British even wanted a piece of Afghanistan. During the mid-nineteenth century, the English launched a series of invasions into the country, which they coveted for its wealth of barren rocks. The English forces attacked with their infamous Brown Bess muskets, and the Afghans responded by stealing those muskets and making their very own firearms from the pieces. This Afghan specialty was known as the *jezail*. Though its firing mechanism was scavenged from British guns, the rest of the jezail was purely Afghani. The handmade stock was often intricately decorated by local artisans, and it featured a distinctive curve not found in any other musket. This would seem to suggest that it was fired under the arm instead of pressed against the shoulder. The barrel of the jezail was also quite long, giving it more range than the Brown Bess. This would ultimately be the demise of the British forces, who were repeatedly ambushed and picked off by Afghan rebels from high clifftops. By the end of the First Anglo-Afghan War, the British had lost tens of thousands of men to their very own firearm mechanisms. Good show, old boy!

USED BY: Middle Eastern soldiers of the nineteenth century
AVAILABLE IN: Smoothbore or rifled
ADVANTAGES: Considerable range; able to shoot from under the arm, which could come in handy on horseback
DISADVANTAGES: Holding the jezail under the arm puts firing mechanism close to user's face, allowing sparks to fly into his eyes

SUMPITAN

Yes, yes, I know. I've already covered blowguns in this book. But the *sumpitan* of Borneo deserves special recognition. This isn't the sly, concealable peashooter of the Japanese ninja. The people of Borneo relied heavily on the sumpitan for survival, so they didn't fuck around with things that resembled drinking straws. When early English conquerors first encountered the Dayaks, they scoffed at their primitive breath-powered weapons. But the English soon stopped scoffing when the Dayaks picked off thirty of their men with sumpitan darts. These blowguns were about seven feet long, made from hardwood, and typically came equipped with a bayonet-like spear tip. (You know . . . for stabbing.) They were remarkably accurate—more so than the firearms of the time—using tiny slivers of bamboo or palm trees as darts. Physically, the wound of the sumpitan dart was almost insignificant. The enemy might think he'd been bitten by a big mosquito at worst. But these tiny, insignificant darts were poisoned with the milky sap of the upas tree, one of the most toxic substances found in the plant kingdom. The dart only had to break the skin, and the fight was over. The upas poison would take effect, shutting down the victim's respiratory system in mere seconds. Think of the sumpitan dart as a cobra that you can throw at people.

EASE
OF USE: ★★★ (wielder must have the lungs of a tuba player)
USED WITH: Upas tree poison
FAMOUS VICTIMS: The party of an English officer known simply as Mr. Johnson, who lost thirty men to sumpitan darts
ADVANTAGES: Can be wielded from thick foliage; remarkably accurate; target dies almost instantly
DISADVANTAGES: Poor range; poison has a short shelf life
"FWWOOOMP!": The last sound you hear before the sumpitan kills you

Chapter 14.

'MERICA!

EATING POSSUM &
SHITTING FREEDOM

1776–1900

BACK IN 1776, a bunch of guys in powdered wigs gathered in Philadelphia and wrote a letter to the king of England. These colonists told the king what he could do with his taxes. Turns out the king of England didn't like shoving money up his rectum. Instead, he sent his army to the colonies and said, "Why don't you say that to my army's face?!" Well, the colonists did exactly that. They fought the King of England's army and kicked their lily-white asses, and a brand-new country called America was born. The skies parted, the railroads were built, and corn was invented. People wore coonskin hats, ate junk food, and shit freedom! (And corn!) They also did an assload of killing along the way.

BOWIE KNIFE

Baseball. Apple pie. And GM Chrysler. These are things that make every red-blooded American warm and tingly inside. And then there's the Bowie knife—that iconic blade of the pioneer that out-Americans everything. It can destroy a baseball, slice up an apple pie, and turn a Chrysler inside out. You could even use it for more reasonable things, like skinning and butchering animals. But this knife is most renowned for its use in fights, like the one involving its namesake Jim Bowie. Bowie was involved in a multi-person duel on a sandbar near Natchez, Mississippi. Though he was shot, stabbed, and beaten to within a breath of Hades, Bowie eventually won the duel with his large butcher knife. From this point on, any large American combat knife was referred to as a Bowie knife, especially the ones with large clip points (where the blade suddenly narrows, as though a large chunk were taken out of it). A couple of years after the sandbar duel, Bowie got another opportunity to use his knife in Texas, when a man he spared in that duel sent three hitmen after him. Even though the assassins had guns, Bowie still wedged his foot firmly up their asses. This time he spared no one, decapitating one guy and disemboweling another. The third man ran away with a massive head wound, never to be heard from again. At this point, Jim Bowie may have gotten a little too sure of himself. He would die at the Battle of the Alamo, his knife unable to save him from the hordes of Mexican troops that had come to take his title of "Mas Macho."

DATE OF ORIGIN: Circa 1829

INVENTED BY: Arkansas blacksmith James Black, with help from Jim Bowie

ALSO CALLED: Arkansas toothpick

FAMOUS VICTIMS: Major Norris Wright, who was stabbed to death by Bowie on the sandbar. Had he won the duel, we might be talking about the "Major Norris Wright knife" instead.

THE KENTUCKY RIFLE

This firearm is often thought of as the first truly original American weapon, but it was actually German colonists who brought it to the States in the early 1700s. Originally known as American longrifles, these guns were different from the smoothbore variety in that they had spiral-shaped grooves carved inside their barrels. This is what made the bullets of the American longrifle spin like the tight spiral of a well-thrown football. The spinning made the projectile more stable in flight. This meant it could fly much farther and straighter than the bullet of a British smoothbore, which lobbed its shot the way an English schoolgirl throws rose petals. This lone firearm didn't exactly win the Revolutionary War for the Americans, but the longrifle, combined with the American frontiersman's buckskin clothing, burned a striking image in the minds of the British. This was the weapon of possum-eating hicks from the backwoods of the Appalachian Mountains. The "lobsterbacks" (British troops) would become utterly terrified of the American riflemen who could put bullets in their eye sockets from two hundred yards. This made the Brits tentative in battle, and Americans would soon win their freedom to marry their cousins and eat possum without being taxed by the king. Now that's fucking freedom.

BIRTHPLACE: Lancaster, Pennsylvania (go figure)
ALSO CALLED: Pennsylvania rifle; American longrifle; "hog rifle"
FAMOUS VICTIMS: The British at the Battle of King's Mountain; the British at the Battle of New Orleans in the War of 1812
ADVANTAGES: Barrel is longer than most previous rifles, giving it longer range; smaller caliber saves precious lead
DISADVANTAGES: Takes longer to load than a smoothbore musket due to the tightness of the rifled barrel

MORTARS

It wasn't long before somebody figured out the limitations of solid cannonballs. They could blast holes in walls, which was all well and good, but where the hell were the explosions? People began to wonder: "What if we hollow out the cannonball, fill it with gunpowder, and develop some sort of fuse that blows the thing up just as it's landing?" Through trial and error, the first timed artillery fuses were developed in the late seventeenth century. This was even harder than it sounded. Bombs that weren't timed properly could easily explode before they were launched, which could ruin a cannon operator's day. They couldn't be used with a traditional high-powder cannon either, as this would destroy the bomb casing before it ever got to the target. That's where the mortar came to the rescue. This special low-velocity cannon was designed specifically to lob exploding artillery at a 45-degree angle. This enabled the projectile to be launched over troublesome obstacles like forests and walls before exploding on the other side. But in order to pull this off, you needed a team of highly educated geometry nerds to accurately predict the trajectory of the mortar shell. You also needed a buttload of slide rules and graph paper, which were not easy to come by in the colonies. America had to make its first run to Staples.

EASE OF USE: ★★★★
(needs math nerds)
SIMILAR TO:
Howitzer, which fires at a slightly lower trajectory than the mortar
ADVANTAGES: Can launch explosive "shells" over enemy fortifications
DISADVANTAGES: This means you might not get to see the explosion

DERRINGER

By the turn of the nineteenth century, people were getting fed up with the flintlock firing mechanism. It misfired, it couldn't be used in the rain, and it suffered from a delay between ignition and firing. Americans were busy making America, and they didn't have time for all that bullshit. In the 1830s, the new percussion cap mechanism took the United States by storm. It featured a hammer that struck a metallic cap filled with fulminate of mercury (some poisonous exploding stuff). Though it took forever for percussion caps to catch on in military circles, they immediately found favor as personal firearms. Right around the same time, a Philadelphia gunsmith named Henry Deringer (the actual spelling) began making small, single-shot pistols that were as big as a person's palm. These pistols were relatively weak. In fact, the bullet of the derringer moved so slowly that you could allegedly see it in flight. Nevertheless, these adorable tiny firearms caught on like wildfire, especially with ladies, who could stuff them in their garter belts or coat pockets just in case some jerk tried to get fresh. Gamblers, ministers, politicians, and anyone else who needed a concealed firearm turned to the derringer for secret protection. It could even be carried inconspicuously into a crowded theater, which is exactly why John Wilkes Booth used it to assassinate Abraham Lincoln.

EASE OF USE: ★★

ADVANTAGES: Easily concealed in a purse or pocket; definite killing power at close range

DISADVANTAGES: Pain in the ass to load; most models only fire one shot; shot is relatively weak, moving at about half the speed of a normal bullet

FUN FACT: Some derringers were made with two barrels, one on top of the other, allowing them to fire two shots before reloading

COLT REVOLVER

Also in the 1830s, a bright young huckster named "Dr. Coult" was traveling around North America giving seminars on chemistry. He wasn't a real doctor, or even a real chemist, but he was a man with a dream. That dream was to make a percussion cap pistol with a revolving chamber that didn't require manual rotation. The dreamer was none other than Samuel Colt, American legend-to-be. His invention didn't really catch on until the 1840s, when the Texas Rangers needed help fighting the Comanche Indians. The old single-shot firearms required twenty valuable seconds to reload. These seconds were costly, often resulting in the shooter catching a Comanche arrow in his neck. Mr. Colt came along and said, "Here's my revolver, which can fire five or six shots without having to reload, all in the convenient body of a small sidearm." Texas said, "Are you fucking kidding me?! Sold!" General Zachary Taylor ordered a big supply. The American West was all but already won.

DATE OF ORIGIN: 1836

SIMILAR TO: The pepperbox pistol, which had a revolving barrel and crazy-bad accuracy

ADVANTAGES: Fires five or six shots without reloading; pulling hammer back rotates barrel, so you don't have to turn it by hand; skilled users can shoot by "fanning" the hammer with their free hand

DISADVANTAGES: Killing Indians will result in centuries of white guilt

FUN FACT: Later Colt models brought the revolver to a new level with their double-action mechanics. These guns featured a barrel that was rotated and fired by a single pull of the trigger, making gunplay even more economical.

EARLY SUBMERSIBLES

If anyone ever asks you if you'd like to go for a ride in a Civil War submarine, your answer should be a resounding "Hellllll no!" These early submersibles may have broken new technological ground, but they were floating death traps. The first one ever to be used in warfare was an American invention known as the *Turtle*. This was essentially a wooden orb piloted by a single passenger. Its torpedo was a simple keg of powder that was to be fastened to the hull of British ships during the Revolutionary War. Even George Washington was skeptical of the *Turtle*, and he turned out to be right, as it never succeeded in blowing anything up. The next attempt at sub warfare came during the Civil War, when the Union army built a submersible called the *Alligator* to take on Confederate ironclad ships. The *Alligator* was a thirty-foot iron tube that was initially propelled by hand-powered oars, and later by a hand-cranked propeller. After miserably failing a series of test runs, the *Alligator* sank to the bottom of the ocean, never to be seen again. Then came the *H. L. Hunley*, the steam-powered submarine of the Confederacy. It required a crew of eight men tightly packed together in the narrow iron hull. In its test drives, the *Hunley* sank twice, killing all crew members. But it was raised from the water both times and recovered. The *Hunley* just wouldn't give up—like an underwater kamikaze version of The Little Engine That Could. Then, in 1864, the *Hunley* accomplished something—it became the first submersible to ever sink a ship, taking out the USS *Housatonic* by explosive charge. Of course, the *Hunley* immediately sank afterwards and asphyxiated all of its crew members yet again, but it had finally proven that perseverance pays off.

USED BY: Americans during the Revolutionary War; Union and Confederate troops during the Civil War

ADVANTAGES: Can theoretically navigate enemy waters without being detected

DISADVANTAGES: Will probably sink and kill everyone on board

GATLING GUN

As if the Civil War wasn't bloody and gruesome enough, the waning years of the conflict saw the introduction of the Gatling gun—a hand-cranked conveyor of rapid-fire death. Any time this multibarreled menace was wheeled onto the battlefield, it would only be a matter of seconds before every man, animal, tree, and rock was reduced to ribbons. Thanks to a gravity-fed ammunition supply, the Gatling fed itself new bullets as it shot. All the shooter had to do was turn its crank and the gun's barrels would rotate, producing a continuous barrage of neverending hellfire. Although it saw limited action in the American Civil War, the Gatling gun was used extensively in the Spanish-American War of 1898. There, it became a favorite weapon of Colonel Teddy Roosevelt, providing him with a very "big stick" indeed. The irony of the Gatling gun: its inventor, Richard Gatling, claimed to have created it to reduce the number of troops committed in combat and make war so horrifying and absolute that it would become futile. In other words, the Gatling gun was his attempt to end wars. Just like how nuclear weapons were made to end nuclear war.

EASE OF USE: ★ﾉ

AVAILABLE IN: Six- and ten-barrel models

PRECURSOR TO: The Maxim gun, the world's first true self-powered machine gun

ADVANTAGES: Obliterates everything in its sights with a continuous stream of bullets; rotating barrels allows the gun to cool and prevent overheating

DISADVANTAGES: Tons of smoke; jamming is likely; will *not* actually end wars

MAXIM GUN

Even though the Gatling gun was a terrifying beast of a weapon, it required manual cranking, which meant it wasn't a proper machine gun. The Maxim gun, on the other hand, performed roughly the same function with virtually no manual labor whatsoever. This gave it the distinction of being the first self-powered machine gun ever to be used in combat. Truth be told, it took a tremendous amount of labor—four to six men—to get the Maxim gun into position. But once it was in place, it could be fired by a single person. The gun operated on an impressively efficient system that used the gas of the fired cartridges to feed the next round into the gun. It required no outside power source other than the ammunition itself. While the guy at the trigger had all the fun, the other members of his team had to feed a constant supply of water into the Maxim's built-in cooling system, which kept the gun from bursting into flames. The gun's firepower was worth it. Its shots were more powerful and more plentiful than those of any other gun on the market, including the Gatling gun. Because of this, the British were able to conquer half the planet, bringing tea time to every time zone on Earth. As a poem of the time put it:

"Whatever happens, we have got
The Maxim gun, and they have not."

DATE OF ORIGIN: 1883
INVENTOR: Hiram Maxim, who has nothing to do with *Maxim* magazine
RATE OF FIRE: Six hundred rounds per minute in theory, three hundred rounds per minute in reality
ADVANTAGES: The most powerful firearm of its time, bar none
DISADVANTAGES: Jams like a motherfucker; needs constant supply of water; will eventually lose to Gandhi

INDEX

John O'Bryan was raised by professional whittlers in the backwoods of Western Tennessee. On Sundays, his father worked as a Baptist minister and instilled in him many of the Bible's most important lessons on how to smite people. His mother would read him the *Dungeons & Dragons Monster Manual* when he couldn't sleep. While living in Memphis, he learned to run from the sound of gunfire. He once got stabbed by Cuban teenagers while vacationing in the Caribbean. He cut his writing teeth typing obituaries for Mississippi's most prestigious newspaper and would later abandon his southern roots to write for Hollywood. There, he would use these life lessons to his advantage, writing for shows like Nickelodeon's *Avatar: The Last Airbender* and Disney XD's *Motorcity*. He currently lives in northeast Los Angeles with his two kids, two cats, and thirty-seven crossbows.

Chronicle Books publishes distinctive books and gifts. From award-winning children's titles, best-selling cookbooks, and eclectic pop culture to acclaimed works of art and design, stationery, and journals, we craft publishing that's instantly recognizable for its spirit and creativity. Enjoy our publishing and become part of our community at www.chroniclebooks.com.